The Deckers have hit ano
aged to translate their po~~pular book, Doing~~
Did, into a manual for small groups in churches of every
size. The material in *Holy Spirit Empowered Small Groups*
is already breathing new life into our congregation. We
have been doing "minichurch" since 1976, but somehow
never fully infused the power of the Spirit into our tool-
kit. All this is changing, due to this material.

John and Sonja overcome our tendency to compart-
mentalize the things of the Spirit. They not only give
practical examples, they give practical assignments. In
short, they make it easy for people to *practice* the things
of the Spirit. With practice comes confidence. That confidence results in miracles at the hands and words of
ordinary Christians. This book will transform you and
your church. It will empower and enthuse your members. My advice—read it together in every small group in
your congregation. It is *not* "just another new thing," but
the ancient church in fresh clothing. This one will mark
your church for years to come!

—RALPH MOORE
PASTOR, NEW HOPE CHAPEL KENEOHE BAY, HAWAII
FOUNDER OF THE HOPE CHAPEL MOVEMENT
AUTHOR OF *STARTING A NEW CHURCH*

The Bible teaches us that the initial community of Christ-
followers met often in small groups. These small groups,
these little platoons, formed the backbone of an authentic community of believers which turned the world on
its ear.

If the church is to once again be a cultural thermostat
(affecting the culture) and not just a cultural thermometer
(reflecting the culture), she must once again become Bible
based, Spirit empowered, and small group reinforced!

John and Sonja Decker have a passion for life-change
in the context of small groups. They are gifted, Spirit-led
small group leaders here at Westside Church. Their group

is a dynamic, reproductive mini-Book-of-Acts community! Their small group has birthed many others, and these dynamic offspring display the same enthusiasm, excitement, and transformative power as the parent group. In their stirring new book, *Holy Spirit Empowered Small Groups*, they explain in practical terms how little communities can become launch pads for bondage-breaking, risk-taking, difference-making, culture-shaking Christians.

—KEN JOHNSON
SENIOR PASTOR, WESTSIDE CHURCH
BEND, OREGON

For quite some time, I have been urging John and Sonja to get this book written as soon as possible! Why? First, because my wife, Jettie, and I have personally experienced the Holy Spirit-empowered group that meets in John and Sonja Decker's home. There we met many of the wonderful "stories" that are recounted in this remarkably practical and encouraging book. There we encountered the living God as He moved among the people in the power of the Holy Spirit. There I experienced physical healing as the Lord precisely identified the location and nature of my condition (tendonitis) through a word of knowledge given to one of the men present. As this man and others prayed for me, a strange warmth flowed over my left arm, and the pain I had carried for several weeks melted away! Needless to say, that made an impression on this sometimes "doubting Thomas"!

A second reason I have awaited this book's completion is that it fills an increasingly urgent need for a proven, easily reproducible model for small groups that releases the huge potential latent in believers just waiting to learn how to do what Jesus did. So here it is: a book that pulsates with encouragement via the stories of *real* people who *really* learned to be doing what Jesus did, and a book with simple, clear guidelines that are proven to work. Thanks, John and Sonja, for a tool that makes

John 14:12 attainable for *any* believer who will be part of a group where the Holy Spirit leads and empowers!

—Dr. Tom Wymore
District Supervisor
Foursquare West Texas

This book is filled with great stories of the Spirit's life-changing and gospel-extending work when He is recognized and allowed to work in our small group communities. You will enjoy, be challenged and inspired by what God can do when He is invited into our small group meetings. The Deckers offer great eye-openers for how Jesus wants to grace His body to build itself up and powerfully reach others in His name.

—Dr. Jim Hayford Sr.
Senior Pastor
Eastside Foursquare Church
Bothell, Washington

John and Sonja Decker's *Holy Spirit Empowered Small Groups* is a practical and fascinating sequel to their first book, *Doing What Jesus Did*. It is an excellent manual on how to provide "small group practicums" for doing what Jesus did in the power of the Holy Spirit—healing the sick, setting captives free, releasing the oppressed, and binding up the brokenhearted. This little book describes the big things God does in small groups through ordinary Christians empowered by His Spirit.

—Dr. John L. Amstutz
Missions Trainer and Consultant
Foursquare Missions International
Fresno, California

"Small groups" and "cell groups" are encouraged in every Christian denomination, yet many small groups of believers become nothing more than a friendship gathering or a pie social. Jesus had something more in mind when He gathered His small group of disciples together. In the New Testament, whenever a few believers were gathered in His name, lives were changed because of the presence of His miraculous Spirit.

I have known John and Sonja Decker for many years and have seen the results of their teaching and their book *Doing What Jesus Did*. Now the Deckers have written a manual that translates into practical knowledge for those leading small groups—a manual that comes out of many years of leading small groups in their own home.

Holy Spirit Empowered Small Groups is a manual which is not ethereal or wishful, but which gives inspiration for the kind of life-changing contact with others which is an obtainable goal. Many issues of spiritual growth cannot be accomplished in a large corporate gathering, but rather in a small group that is heart-warming and heart-changing, whose leaders understand the principles which the Deckers present so clearly in this new book.

—DR. CLIFF HANES
FOURSQUARE MISSIONS INTERNATIONAL

John and Sonja Decker's manual for small group discipleship, *Holy Spirit Empowered Small Groups*, is a how-to guide for leading and developing spiritually effective fellowship. They have developed a step-by-step leadership guide for teaching groups to minister in spiritual power and healing gifts.

Reflecting a Pentecostal approach to Spirit-baptism, this manual will enable local church and small group leaders to train and inspire Christians to develop small groups that address issues of healing, addictions, and other spiritual ministries from a biblically-based perspective.

While their approach may raise questions from within the traditional evangelical theological point of view, they have shown how these spiritual ministry issues may be addressed within the context of accountability to the church and orthodox Christian faith. Their emphasis on leadership accountability and spiritual discernment, as well as spiritual maturity, is a critical need in this time of profound superficiality in much of our culture, and, unfortunately, in many churches, as well. For those seeking a strong emphasis on ministry in the Spirit, this is an excellent resource.

—R. LARRY SHELTON, TH.D.
RICHARD B. PARKER PROFESSOR OF THEOLOGY
GEORGE FOX EVANGELICAL SEMINARY
NEWBERG, OREGON

HOLY SPIRIT
EMPOWERED
SMALL GROUPS

HOLY SPIRIT EMPOWERED SMALL GROUPS

JOHN AND SONJA DECKER

Foursquare Media

Holy Spirit Empowered Small Groups
by John and Sonja Decker
Published by Foursquare Media
1910 W. Sunset Blvd., Suite 200
Los Angeles, California 90026

This book is produced and distributed by Creation House, a part of Strang Communications, www.creationhouse.com.

All scripture quotations are from *The New King James Version* (NKJV) unless otherwise noted. Copyright ©1979, 1980, 1982, by Thomas Nelson, Inc., publishers. Used by permission.

All scripture quotations in Appendix A are from *The Holy Bible, New International Version.* Copyright © 1973, 1978, 1984 by International Bible Society. Used by permission of Zondervan. All rights reserved.

Cover design by Terry Clifton

Library of Congress Control Number: 2006933869
International Standard Book Number–10: 1-59979-083-1
International Standard Book Number–13: 978-1-59979-083-1

First Edition

06 07 08 09 10 — 9 8 7 6 5 4 3 2 1
Printed in the United States of America

Acknowledgments

Thanks…

To the original "small group"—Father, Son, and Holy Spirit.

To the International Church of the Foursquare Gospel, our church family, and its president, Dr. Jack W. Hayford. If only all busy, important servant-leaders would so clearly demonstrate such humble servanthood as you have.

To Ken Johnson, senior pastor, Westside Church, Bend, Oregon, who has allowed us to live out the principles in this book in the life of our local church.

To Ralph Moore, senior pastor, Hope Chapel Kaneohe Bay in Hawaii, who has inspired us and countless others with his humble transparency and passion for the mini-church way of life.

To Dr. R. Larry Shelton, professor of theology at George Fox Evangelical Seminary, Newberg, Oregon, who has believed in and encouraged us over the past twenty years.

To Dr. John L. Amstutz, missions trainer and consultant, Foursquare Missions International, Fresno, California, who made time to review this manuscript, and helped keep our theology in the middle of the road.

To Dr. Jim Hayford, Sr., senior pastor, Eastside Foursquare Church, Bothell, Washington, who has been a faithful friend and pastor. He first introduced our Ambassador Series curriculum in the U. S. church.

To Dr. Cliff Hanes, Foursquare Missions International, our

friend who rejoices over our every success and enthusiastically cheers us on to the next assignment.

To Dr. Tom Wymore, district supervisor, Foursquare West Texas, who inspires us by his enthusiasm about the things of the Spirit. Theology and the power of the Holy Spirit have converged in his life. What a joy for us to experience those things with him.

To Greg and Karen Fry and Ray and Gloria Hoffman, our faithful co-laborers who excel us in so many ways. Your friendships enrich our lives. And to think we get to enjoy this life together—with eternity just around the corner!

Contents

Foreword

JOHN AND SONJA Decker have given the church an *igniting* resource—a catapult to launch believers into the full-dimensioned life of a true disciple of Jesus.

Gifted teachers, the Deckers tirelessly pursue the formation of believers-into-disciples. They know that Jesus' plan for His own is not only to bring us unto Father God, but that we might enter His kingdom through the cross. Our Lord's intention is to baptize us with the Holy Spirit, equipping us to expand His kingdom as He multiplies His own anointed ministry through us.

John and Sonja's passion to serve our Lord's vision for His church has resulted in this practical tool kit for establishing disciples as functional, spiritually-prepared representatives of God's kingdom.

Holy Spirit Empowered Small Groups unfolds the simple but dynamic ways that small groups can become a training ground for the shaping and equipping of Spirit-born, Spirit-filled, Spirit-led, Spirit-formed Christians. The model the Deckers present is our Savior's own—the same means that penetrated the ancient world and impacted multitudes (one at a time) with the healing, freeing, saving love of Christ.

Through decades of pastoral ministry, I have sought first to bring newborn children who have been saved in Christ to second, become ignited believers baptized in the Spirit by Christ, and third, to be shaped as equipped disciples who function like Christ. To achieve this, the third step must take place in the small group environment, just as Jesus began with the twelve in His own "small group."

Though small groups are common in much of the church today, many are limited to fellowship, basic Bible study, or mutual care. While these are certainly worthy values, I believe Jesus had something more in mind. When He gathered His own small group of disciples, He was shaping them to receive the promise of the Father. After they had received the gift of the Holy Spirit, they would be empowered, in our Lord's words, to do "the works that I do…and greater than these" (John 14:12).

At the bottom line, this is what discipleship is really about. It begins with God's Word, but it isn't completed until we learn how to do His Son's works. So welcome to this small, but essential resource for real disciples. And welcome to a meeting with two faith stimulators—John and Sonja Decker. You may already know them, but if not, I am pleased to present two such trustworthy leaders, proven faithful servants, compassionate teachers, and anointed communicators to you.

I'm sure you'll find the vibrancy of your life in Christ enhanced for having encountered their help in expanding God's kingdom and enlarging your own walk in the Holy Spirit.

—JACK W. HAYFORD
PRESIDENT, INTERNATIONAL FOURSQUARE CHURCHES
CHANCELLOR, THE KING'S COLLEGE AND SEMINARY
FOUNDING PASTOR, THE CHURCH ON THE WAY

Introduction

ALONG WITH MANY Christians around our world, we are praying for a spiritual awakening that will sweep millions of people into God's kingdom. Sometimes, however, we can't help but wonder what will happen when our prayer is answered. How will these new converts be cared for, nurtured, and discipled? The American church seems ill prepared for such an event.

It is our prayer that this small book you hold in your hands—written by both of us, but set down in my (Sonja's) voice—will in some small way contribute to the solution. Jesus Himself chose a small group of twelve to mentor, and then committed His church into the care of eleven of them. He instructed them to wait to begin their work after they were empowered with the Holy Spirit. After that watershed event in Acts 2:1–4, the believers met in the temple courts…and in homes (vv. 46–47).

So continuing daily with one accord in the temple, and breaking of bread from house to house, they ate their food with gladness and simplicity of heart, praising God and having favor with all the people. And the Lord added to the church daily those who were being saved.

If we in our local churches today would be deliberate about using this model, we could raise up Spirit-filled leaders to help shoulder the tremendous responsibility and workload in growing churches. There are vast, untapped "people resources" in our churches that need to be identified, retooled, and mobilized. Let's begin now to prepare for the answer to our prayer for this glorious end-time harvest.

Speaking of that harvest and the urgent need for laborers, Matthew wrote:

> Then Jesus went about all the cities and villages, teaching in their synagogues, preaching the gospel of the kingdom, and healing every sickness and every disease among the people. But when He saw the multitudes, He was moved with compassion for them, because they were weary and scattered, like sheep having no shepherd. Then He said to His disciples, "The harvest truly is plentiful, but the laborers are few. Therefore pray the Lord of the harvest to send out laborers into His harvest."
> —MATTHEW 9:35–38

One of the ways we can begin to earnestly prepare for a great ingathering of souls in our nation is to train workers who can teach, preach, and heal the sick like Jesus did. Here's a simple plan that has been used for over twenty years to effectively train leaders:

Establish a small group-based training center in the local church that will effectively equip Christians to minister in the power of the Holy Spirit.

Using the MTC graduates, form small groups, mini-churches, or cells where people can experience the authentic, biblical power of the Holy Spirit. These groups naturally create interest in the attendees for more training, sparking further interest in MTCs. They enroll, graduate, and form more groups—and the Holy Spirit-perpetuated organic growth cycle continues. The MTC also helps people discover their giftedness and passion, facilitating expanded ministry in all departments of the church—and out into the wider world.

While the average Christian has little inclination or opportunity to go to Bible school or seminary, many are eager to be better equipped for ministry. It has been our observation that many in-church training programs or institutes are too academic for the average church attendee. If, however, we marry the teaching to firsthand experience in a small-group practicum, people will come. We see little attrition in our MTC from September to May. The secret is in the hands-on training. Shortly after moving to Bend, Oregon, and becoming part of the Westside family, we began a home group with just five people. This book chronicles the spiritual growth in those lives, and in the life of our church.

SHERI'S STORY

How would you like to belong to a small group where week in and week out people are healed, and set free from long-term habits and bondages? Would you go home each week just a little encouraged and excited?

Here is how our friend Sheri recalled the experience:

> I began attending a small group at John and Sonja Decker's, and was soon praying with other believers and "doing what Jesus did." Weekly, my husband heard my wonderful stories of people being healed and helped by the Lord in their various trials. We invited the Deckers and others from the group to our home for a barbeque so my husband could meet them on his own turf. He wasn't sure just what he thought about all of this healing and deliverance stuff.
>
> After that evening, he decided that he, too, would attend the group and become an integral part. During this time God impressed my husband and me to pray and agree for sixty days that He would bring our prodigal son home. He had been lost and using drugs for about eight years. We were diligent in our prayers, and when

we asked our son to come home with the stipulation that he become drug free, attend our church, and the church recovery group, we were shocked to learn that the Holy Spirit had prepared his heart to agree!

Our son settled into a new life and was intrigued by our accounts of miracles and wonders in our small group. He said he would also like to come along. The love of God and the power of the Holy Spirit moved him week after week. Summer flew by and our sixty days of covenant prayer with the Lord ended. The next night all three of us attended John and Sonja's small group for a powerful evening of worship and prayer, healings and restoration of lives.

At the end of our evening, my husband and I watched in amazement as John was led by the Spirit to ask our son if he needed prayer. In awe we saw God fulfill His great promise of salvation for our son. God had restored and redeemed our prodigal son in less than twenty-four hours following the completion of the sixty days of prayer!

We believe the small group gathering in the loving power of the Holy Spirit was a direct result of God's mercy to our son and to us.

Soon after, Jeff was baptized in water. And when I spoke recently in a Wednesday evening service on leading a Holy Spirit empowered life, Ken and Jeff, father and son, both responded to be baptized in the Holy Spirit. They received this gift and, for the first time, prayed in their spiritual languages.[1]

The next morning I called their home. Ken answered the phone, and said they were having a joyous family prayer time, celebrating God's goodness. Ken and Sheri have continued to flourish in our home group. He has recently learned to play the guitar, and they now lead worship each Tuesday evening at our gathering. When we are out of town, they lead for us, and do a fabulous job.

This is the very type of experience new believers encountered in the Book of Acts, and it was unlike anything they had ever witnessed. After Jesus' death, burial, resurrection, and ascension, these excited new Christians were empowered by His Holy Spirit to do the very same things He did.

> Most assuredly, I say to you, he who believes in Me, the works that I do he will do also; and greater works than these he will do, because I go to My Father.
>
> —JOHN 14:12

That first beautiful blossoming of the early church met in the temple courts and from house to house, as the Lord added to the church daily those who were being saved (see Acts 2:46). *We believe that it was the close-knit relationships in the home meetings that bonded these believers.*

It's no different today. People who experience the living God in this radical way just naturally want to share the Good News with their family, friends, neighbors, and coworkers. Sometimes these guests visit at a home group before attending an actual service at the church building.

Holy Spirit empowered small groups are essential for authentic New Testament Christianity. The flock cannot be adequately cared for by a church leadership and staff—not without burning them out! As any pastor or church leader will tell you, people's needs can be overwhelming. Physical, mental, emotional, and relational catastrophes are becoming more and more acute as our postmodern culture reaps what it has sown.

When asked about the signs of the end of the age, Jesus told His followers that because of the increase of lawlessness, the love of many would grow cold, but the one who stood firm to the end would be saved (see Matthew 24:12–13). Who can watch the evening news week after week without being stunned by the increase of cruelty and wickedness? Man's inhumanity to his fellow man is staggering. We are daily shocked with around-the-world accounts of brutal regimes torturing their own people, terrorists killing innocent civilians, serial killers, and even children gunning down their classmates in demonic acts of hatred and revenge. People are beaten down under the emotional battering they receive day after day.

PLACES OF REFUGE AND SAFETY

Yes, it can be a cold, dark, oppressive world out there. But here is where the Christian church through Holy Spirit empowered small groups intersects society and human need. It is God's brilliant way to shepherd His beloved people. These dynamic home groups are to be places of refuge and safety—an environment providing love, acceptance, and forgiveness in a society full of hate, rejection, and unforgiveness.

No matter how sincere our intentions or desires, we simply cannot be cared for or discipled in a congregational setting alone. Those gatherings are for teaching, celebration, and motivation. For the most part, people sitting around us in the church service will not even be aware of our personal circumstances. We may be in intense agony with nowhere to turn, yet we often walk out through those church doors in the same condition that we walked in. If, however, someone engages us in deliberate conversation, lovingly inquires about us, and invites us to their small group, we will find our opportunity for support and healing. One of the key phrases to include in the invitation is, "It's a safe place."

One Wednesday evening at Westside Church, Pastor Ken called us aside before the service, and said he would like to introduce us to a couple. Contemplating marriage, they were working through some very tough issues of previous marriages, lifestyles, children, and their faith.

After talking for a short while with Richard and Andrea (not their real names), we felt the way we could best help them would be for them to join our weekly Tuesday evening home group. We invited them to the next meeting and explained how they would see healthy and respectful marriages among those attending. The couples were by no means perfect, we hastened to add, but they were growing both individually and as marriage partners. We said it was a loving, accepting, and safe place, so they agreed to visit the following week.

Spirit Baptism

By the couple's second visit, Andrea said she wanted to be baptized in the Holy Spirit, enabling her to pray in a spiritual language as with others in the group. When John saw her resolve, he made sure she understood that this gift, like salvation, was hers for the asking. The only prerequisites are that the person is truly in a personal relationship with the Lord Jesus Christ, and that he or she is hungry for more of God—desiring the supernatural power of God that is released in this experience.

Andrea definitely met the prerequisites, so John led her in a simple prayer. Immediately, she received the gift and her prayer language. She began to laugh, cry, and pray all at the same time. As it turned out, she would need that new dimension in her life to make the very difficult decisions she would face in the months to come.

She came faithfully every week, and seemed to be in awe as people were healed by prayer before her very eyes. Richard, the man she was considering marrying, did not desire to walk this path she was choosing, and they mutually agreed to postpone their wedding plans. Eventually, they decided marriage was not an option. The group in no way pressured Andrea into such decisions. We simply loved and encouraged her as she and the Lord worked out the healthy path He set before her.

Ministry Training

Our church's Ministry Training Center (MTC) was beginning in September, and Andrea asked about attending. We explained that it was for those who were serious about becoming effective marketplace Christians. It was quite a commitment for a single mom, because the class is a nine-month MTC that meets every

Monday night for three hours. The training is small-group based, and has proven to be extremely beneficial for people like herself who hunger to learn more. She prayed about it and came back with the strong assurance that she was to move forward.

In the beginning she felt extremely inferior and inadequate, especially during the small group practicum sessions where all students are expected to participate. More than once she thought she would quit, but we kept encouraging her to remain in the class. Finally, she had a breakthrough in using Scripture in her prayers. Before long she was operating in revelation knowledge through the Holy Spirit, and began to see people healed as she prayed for them.

Andrea was on her way! We get phone calls almost every week from her, relating how she has had opportunity to pray for people in her marketplace.

One of the precious things about Andrea is her heart of submission and willingness to be instructed. She appreciates feedback, and on numerous occasions has asked us to tell her if she says or does anything inappropriate. Very seldom, if ever, have we needed to do this. She has been a quick learner and brought John and me much joy.

Duck and Ducklings

One Sunday after the service at church, Andrea came to us for prayer for her four children's salvation. While we were praying, I saw a picture in my mind of a mama duck swimming in a pond. There were four ducklings swimming out in the marsh among the reeds. As the mama duck kept swimming straight ahead, one by one the ducklings fell in line behind her.

Andrea cried like a baby and tucked the promise away in her heart. Her oldest was a Marine, who came home on leave before shipping out to the battlefront in Kosovo. Impressed by the changes he saw in his mother, he agreed to come to home group with her.

As the meeting began, he sat very stiff and erect on the leather sofa next to his mom. When John asked him if there was anything he would like us to pray about, he said, "Yes sir—that all my buddies would return home safe and sound." He didn't ask anything for himself. When the group prayed, however, we certainly included him in our prayers.

Later, while other prayer ministry was going on in another part of the room, I quietly slipped over and sat on the arm of the sofa next to him. "We have prayed for you and your buddies to be safe," I said to him, "but if something were to happen to you while you are over there, do you know where you would spend eternity?"

"No, ma'am, I don't," he said.

"Would you like to settle that issue tonight? Would you like to invite Jesus Christ into your heart and have all your sins forgiven?"

"Yes, ma'am, I would."

I led him in a simple salvation prayer that he repeated after me. Neither of us anticipated what happened next. The Holy Spirit came upon him in such power that he began to visibly shake all over.

"May I ask you a question, ma'am?"

"Of course," I replied.

"Why am I shaking when I'm not cold?"

I explained that that was the presence of the Holy Spirit of God, signifying to him that this was real.

He came back to our home the afternoon before he left, was baptized in the Holy Spirit, and received a beautiful supernatural prayer language. God was pleased to answer our prayers, and this young man's division completed their tour of duty and returned to the U. S. without a single casualty or serious injury.

A GROUP OF HER OWN

When our church studied Rick Warren's *Forty Days of Purpose*, Andrea approached us with the desire to host a group in her home. We knew she was ready, and encouraged her to do so. She began with ten people, but by the end of the forty days there were twenty-four attending. Praying just like she learned at our home group and the ministry training center, she has also taught her group to pray.

Because of the dramatic answers to prayers, people began to bring their friends. When the "Forty Days of Purpose" group finally disbanded, Andrea went on to birth yet another small group—this one "for women only."

In fourteen months Andrea has gone from being a worldly baby Christian with her life in shambles to a responsible, loving mother and an effective small group leader.

WHAT IT'S ALL ABOUT

We began our home group in 1998 when we moved to Bend, Oregon, and joined Westside Church. As far as we can recall, the members of our small group have not needed to take personal problems and concerns to the pastoral staff for ministry—they have received loving care and true discipleship from each and every member of the group. It's not a "John and Sonja thing"—it is every individual in our Tuesday night gathering supplying what the others need. It is a true expression of the body ministering to itself as Paul outlined to the church in Corinth.

> But now indeed there are many members, yet one body. And the eye cannot say to the hand, "I have no need of you;" nor again the head to the feet, "I have no need of you." No, much rather, those members of the body which seem to be weaker are necessary. And those members of the body which we think to be less honorable, on these we bestow greater honor; and our

unpresentable parts have greater modesty, but our presentable parts have no need. But God composed the body, having given greater honor to that part which lacks it, that there should be no schism in the body, but that the members should have the same care for one another. And if one member suffers, all the members suffer with it; or if one member is honored, all the members rejoice with it.

—1 Corinthians 12:20–26

In the context of a loving, safe, Holy Spirit-empowered small group, many are experiencing the miracle of oneness in Jesus Christ. In today's culture, so characterized by loneliness and alienation, that is no small thing.

Chapter 1

Jesus Loves Small Groups

DISCIPLESHIP WORKS BEST in a small group. Jesus' personal small group consisted of twelve men whom He discipled and mentored. The seventy were discipled by observing what Jesus did. He appointed them, and sent them out with much the same instructions as He had given the twelve. The multitudes listened intently to Jesus, but were not discipled.

Were they inspired? Yes. Healed and delivered? Definitely. But not discipled. There were simply too many. Jesus' pattern for proper discipleship began with a small group of a dozen men.

> And when He had called His twelve disciples to Him, He gave them power over unclean spirits, to cast them out, and to heal all kinds of sickness and all kinds of disease.
> —MATTHEW 10:1

> Then He called His twelve disciples together and gave them power and authority over all demons, and to cure diseases. He sent them to preach the kingdom of God and to heal the sick.
> —LUKE 9:1–2

1

> And He called the twelve to Himself, and began to send them out two by two, and gave them power over unclean spirits.
>
> —MARK 6:7

Jesus knew the importance of pouring His life and energy into the twelve. He discipled them by teaching them in a close, relational connection where they could watch, do what He commanded, benefit from immediate feedback, and receive personal correction as needed. Jesus knew these men would in turn disciple the first generation of Christians. And He also knew they would only accomplish that to the extent that they themselves had been discipled.

Mentoring is the key. When we have been discipled in an atmosphere of a close, personal relationship where we are instructed, critiqued, and personally encouraged to do as our mentor is doing, we learn quickly and thoroughly.

No book—no matter how thorough or well-researched—has the teaching power of an instructed, Spirit-filled mentor. In the process of our learning, we can ask personal questions about how to increase our faith, expecting God to work through us. We can watch as our teacher demonstrates how to preach, minister, and pray for the sick. We can observe and ask questions as our mentor encourages us to use our authority to drive out evil spirits. We can do as our teacher does as he or she shows us how to implement the principles of the kingdom of God.

Finally, we are sent out two by two with the expectation of the same results we saw demonstrated by our mentor. Matthew 10:7–8 takes shape in our midst and comes alive: "And as you go, preach, saying, 'The kingdom of heaven is at hand.' Heal the sick, cleanse the lepers, raise the dead, cast out demons. Freely you have received, freely give."

This can only be done when we learn in a small group of twelve or less with leaders who know how to do what Jesus has called us to do. He showed us how to preach to small crowds and to multitudes. When the multitudes came, He instructed His disciples to divide them into small groups and feed them. In doing this, He was starting to show the twelve how to disciple large groups of people—break them into smaller groups where needs can be met and where they can personally learn and apply the principles of the kingdom of God.

THE DISCIPLESHIP CHALLENGE

Large numbers of people are turning to the church as the world races along on its course of ruin and sorrow.

The challenge of today's church is to quickly direct those highly-vulnerable new lambs into effective discipleship. We know many church leaders are concerned when the number of people being "saved" does not match the number being baptized and signing up for new believer's classes. We ask, "What happened to them? Where did they go?"

You would think that truly born-again converts would stick around more than a week or two and start the discipleship process. The larger the crowd, however, the more difficult it is to locate those who raised their hand to investigate salvation in Jesus Christ. We ask ourselves, "Did they truly come to faith? Was having them come down front too invasive? Will they come back next week?"

We ask in the nicest way possible to consider attending our new believer's class. Only a fraction, however, signs up. In a big church where only twelve show up to be discipled, we begin to think our program is a failure. Could the Lord be saying to us, "I discipled twelve. How many do you think you can handle?"

A RADICAL APPROACH

We are suggesting a more radical approach. What if we had fresh testimonies on Sundays from small group leaders who shared authentic, confirmed healings and miracles happening in their midst? What if the people who experienced healing gave personal testimony about how Jesus healed them? What if those testifying invited anyone interested in joining a small group to talk with them after the service?

Pre-Christians are not turned off by the supernatural manifestation of God's power. On the contrary, Jesus demonstrated that this is one of the best ways to evangelize our communities. As we allow the authentic power of God to be shown forth among us, the Holy Spirit will draw greater and greater numbers to our churches.

The multitudes didn't flock to Jesus because of a cleverly designed small group promotion. It was not because someone composed slick announcements in the bulletin or ran a clever video clip on the big screen. Mark 3:8 tells us that "a great multitude, when they heard how many things He was doing, came to Him."

It is not the way we ask or advertise or promote. It is the exciting evidence of our Lord's presence and power that motivates people to come. If what we are doing has an immediate application to a real need in a person's life, you can't keep them away.

Matthew 4:24 says:

> Then His fame went throughout all Syria; and they brought to Him all sick people who were afflicted with various diseases and torments, and those who were demon-possessed, epileptics, and paralytics; and He healed them.

The power of God authenticates the message. Wherever things are happening, people will hear the news and crowd into our gatherings. Healing, of course, is a universal need in every city. Every family has someone who needs to be healed. Many will go anywhere they believe the power of God is being released.

But don't think of television cameras, Christian celebrities, or dynamic platform ministries in big meeting halls. The best place to show forth the power of the living God is in a small group.

Little Platoons

Pastor Ken at Westside often urges us toward a goal of becoming a church *of* small groups, rather than a church *with* small groups. He points out that the Father, Son, and the Holy Spirit were the original "small group." They obviously enjoy one another and work in divine harmony as One.

Another metaphor Pastor Ken uses is "little platoons." We especially like this imagery because it fits with our concept of living life together. Soldiers in a platoon train together, live together, care for one another, and, when needed, go to war together.

In many ways that describes what we experience in our small group. Each week we get a little stronger in our faith. We are incrementally built up, and when needed—when the enemy of our souls attacks one of our number—we move as one and "go to war." There's nothing like having friends who are committed to you through thick and thin, and will encircle you in your time of illness, misfortune, or spiritual battle.

We know the truth of the following proverb: "A man who has friends must himself be friendly, But there is a friend who sticks closer than a brother" (Proverbs 18:24). Jesus clearly modeled the small group concept with the twelve He chose to be with Him. He discipled them, mentored them, empowered them, and then entrusted His work into their hands as they moved in the power of the Holy Spirit. He is our Hero and our Model.

It's interesting to think about one of the twelve being so disloyal that Satan entered him, persuading him to betray the Lord. We need to remember that because, once in a great while, someone will severely disappoint us.

We were created to be a part of God's family. Jesus said: "Again I say to you that if two of you agree on earth concerning anything that they ask, it will be done for them by My Father in heaven. For where two or three are gathered together in My name, I am there in the midst of them" (Matthew 18:19–20).

The Holy Spirit loves to assist us in fellowship with God's family. He is in our midst, giving us His fruit and His gifts to share with each other. This takes many forms: love, joy, peace, healing, encouragement, kindness, helping one another, and praying for each other.

Our culture is so dysfunctional that many people are lonely, confused, and fearful. We have the matchless Good News that God wants them to be a part of His family. Living in koinonia (community) as He intended creates a deep sense of belonging within God's children.

Our small group is a lifeline. The gathering in our home every Tuesday night, year round, is so important to us that we arrange our busy travel schedule so we can be home for the meeting—even taking red-eye flights if necessary.

If John or I have an urgent need, we call one of our group members, not the church office. They know us, they're familiar with our life circumstances, and we bear each other's burdens. We pray for each other before making important decisions, and we minister in practical ways if someone is ill.

Can you identify with what we're describing here? If you're not in a group like this, seek one out. Or start one in your own home!

The Holy Spirit is our honored guest each time we meet, and we invite Him to minister to us through one another. And He always does! He brings that supernatural life and vitality that energizes us when we are in His presence. One night a few months ago, John had each person tell the group what they had brought to share. Some said encouragement, several had a testimony of what God had done, and two said they had faith for healing. We had those two pray for several hurting individuals in our group, and those who were prayed for were healed.

The power for healing within our group has gone beyond easing flu symptoms or aches and pains. We have also seen major, dramatic healings as group members have been set free from long-term fibromyalgia and even torn rotator cuffs. Most of the time, it is the members of the group, not John and Sonja, doing the praying.

THE HIGH PRIVILEGE OF MENTORING

Over the last six years we have had the privilege of mentoring people who have become our true brothers and sisters. We are family. It all started with two married couples and a single lady who lived in the same vicinity where we bought our home.

When I called the single lady and invited her, she seemed quite hesitant. She asked if there were any other single people who would be attending. I responded by asking, "What does that have to do with anything? We'll invite any and everyone, including college students, if we learn of any living in this area." I finally persuaded her by suggesting that she attend the first meeting, and if she felt uncomfortable in any way, she didn't have to come back.

As it turned out, we all seemed to fit together right from the start and began doing life together. None of us have family in the area, so we have become a family. When our dear single lady Janis moved to her new home, we were there—packing, loading, unpacking, and helping her settle in with a house-warming. Over the years, all of us have stayed in her beautiful new home at one time or another. She is such a loving, thoughtful friend and has added much richness to our group over the years. Jewish by descent and tradition, she has given us many insights into our Christian roots in Judaism.

Janis joined our second ministry training center, becoming more and more confident in her faith. She even began a before-school prayer meeting with other teachers at her school. She also serves as a service coordinator in our children's department at our church. What strength and blessing she has brought to her family, to the small group she now hosts, to her coworkers, and to the church. She is totally committed to the concept of personal growth in a loving community.

JESUS OUR HEALER

Greg and Karen, one of the couples in our original group, went through some significant health problems during that first year. He had to resign as administrator at our church because of the debilitating rheumatoid arthritis that seized his body. The last month he was on staff, he couldn't even put on his socks and shoes without his wife's assistance. What a battle for this former rugby player!

Our little group surrounded them in this crisis and stood in faith with them for total healing. It took a year of making some significant lifestyle changes to relieve the stress that had triggered the crippling and degenerative disease. The Lord healed him from the inside out as he faced his fears of rejection and abandonment. Being a people pleaser in an attempt to garner acceptance had eaten him alive, but as the revelations came one by one, he began to heal. He is now 98 percent restored in his physical body and is an inspiration to the people who exercise with him every day at the local fitness center.

Early on, Greg and Karen asked us to mentor them. We felt honored to be asked, and began to bring them alongside us in everything we were doing, including teaching leadership seminars in the U. S. and overseas, and serving wholeheartedly in our local church. We saw God's calling upon this couple's lives and prayed earnestly with them that the Lord would give them clear direction about their future.

PILOT PROGRAMS

The summer after we began our mentoring relationship with Greg and Karen, Greg asked what we thought about their beginning a training center at our local church. Pastor Ken immediately saw the possibilities. He agreed that this would be a great way to launch a pilot program and would demonstrate how people would respond to being in class once a week for nine months.

In fact, the "pilot program" took off like a rocket. The students loved it! For every hour of classroom instruction, we have a half-hour of hands-on practicum in a small group environment. The students learn the following six ministry skills:

- leading people to Christ

- leading Christians into the Holy Spirit baptism

- learning how to heal the sick

- hearing from God

- healing the sick by revelation

- healing people with demons

It was so elating to see the spiritual transformation of those students as the year progressed, and they all gained proficiency in their ministry skills. To graduate, they had to fulfill several marketplace ministry assignments by attempting to:

- lead two pre-Christians into relationship with the Lord;

- pray with two Christians to be baptized in the Holy Spirit;

- pray with two people for healing.

Guess what happened as they ventured out of their comfort zones and made that attempt to minister in the marketplace. They were successful—and very excited! Their enthusiasm stirred interest for the next year's class, and so it has been every year since.

This past year, our church has launched a "Master's Commission" intern program for young people eighteen to twenty-four years old. Twenty Cascade Master's Commission students and leaders joined our class in September, along with forty-five adult students.

Those young people brought a super-charged dynamic into the class. Their worship, energy, curiosity, and commitment were contagious. This intergenerational center raised the love quotient of those sixty-five students, along with the fifteen graduates who serve as small group leaders and members of our teaching team. That's eighty people who bonded beyond all of our expectations because of the Holy Spirit empowered small group practicum sessions every week.

Greg's teaching gift has flourished in this environment, along with several others we added to our teaching team. That's another strong benefit of engaging in small groups— gifts and talents are recognized and released. Let's face it, there just aren't too many opportunities for people to learn how to teach, prophesy, or heal the sick in our churches today.

OPPORTUNITIES TO PRACTICE

Years ago a woman who was on staff at our church asked the senior leader in a staff meeting, "Pastor, where does a good girl get to practice a bad sermon so she can improve?"

That haunting question has stuck with us through the years. We need to provide opportunities in our local churches where we can recognize and release the gifts the Lord has placed in our midst. If we will do that, the church body will be well cared for without overworking our paid staff and putting a strain on their marriages and vital family relationships.

Greg has actually excelled us in how he runs the MTC at Westside Church. His pastoring and training of the small group leaders exceeds what we have done in any of our previous MTCs. This is an excellent way for those graduates to be pastored, and to continue to grow in their leadership gifts.

Greg and Karen now head up Westside Church's entire Prayer Force ministry. At this writing, MTC graduates fill 80 percent of our church's prayer ministry positions. They are dispersed throughout the church in all of the numerous departments and ministries. Trained and well-equipped, they minister with servant-leader hearts. How exciting to see people who are fully committed to the Lord Jesus and His church, assuming more and more responsibility as non-paid staff! True mentors rejoice when their disciples excel them. And we do.

WITHOUT GUILE

The other couple that joined our original group of seven was Dave and Jeannie. We have often said of this couple, "They are without guile." Introverted by temperament, they were quiet and tentative about sharing or praying in a group setting. About the third or fourth week we met together, we were soliciting prayer requests when Dave blurted out, "I have chewed tobacco for twenty-two years and have tried everything I know to quit, but nothing has worked. I have come to realize the Lord Jesus will help me quit, so will you all pray for me?"

He then went on to explain that he worked in the logging industry and ran huge pieces of machinery all day. Chewing was simply a part of the culture—smoking was too dangerous. As we gathered around him to pray, the Holy Spirit spoke to John, revealing to him that Dave's habit was more than just a physical addiction, but that he had opened himself up to a demonic spirit of bondage.

11

Now how do you explain that to someone who has not had any teaching about the supernatural? John simply told him the reason he was unable to quit was because there was a spiritual dimension to the addiction, and we could address that if he truly wanted to be free.

"Do whatever you have to, John," Dave pleaded. "Please! I do want to be free." John simply addressed the spirit of bondage in the name of the Lord Jesus Christ and commanded it to leave Dave. We then prayed for strength and resolve to break the habit.

Dave's deliverance was instantaneous. He was filled with joy! With the exception of one small relapse a couple of months later, he has been tobacco free for over six years. Now that's practical Christianity! The devastation of his brief relapse brought him to total repentance—and an even greater commitment to the small group.

Dave and Jeannie were in the first MTC we graduated here at our church in Bend. They are gifted small group leaders in the MTC, lead another small group, and also serve in numerous other ministries in our fellowship. Jeannie has become a powerful intercessor. We had the privilege of seeing this gift birthed in her by the Holy Spirit. She continues to amaze us with her spiritual discernment, commitment, prophetic prayers, and faith. This lovely, shy woman even led our church's National Day of Prayer service with grace and a strong anointing. She also teaches in a para-church organization that helps women transition from prison to meaningful lives in our community.

How rewarding it is to see people transformed before our very eyes. This couple may have been overlooked if they had not chosen to become part of a loving and safe small group. As confident MTC graduates, they now function as steady, faithful leaders.

Yes, Jesus loves small groups, and when they are Holy Spirit empowered, He does some exciting things through the people who gather in His name. In the next chapter we will explore just how we go about creating an atmosphere that invites His presence and fellowship.

Chapter 2

Let's Do It Jesus' Way

WHEN IT CAME to mentoring His disciples, the Lord Jesus had a method: a small group.

Our personal experience in small groups has proven the concept worked even when we didn't have a clue as to what we were doing!

After I was baptized in the Holy Spirit, I was so transformed that my family and friends wanted to spend time with me and learn about what I was experiencing. They all began to come to my home on Saturday mornings. What thrilling days those were! We invited pre-Christians, and they accepted the Lord. Then we showed them in the Bible how they could be empowered by the Holy Spirit, receiving a special prayer language that would enable them to pray in God's will more effectively (see Romans 8:27).

They had only to ask for the gift, and they would receive it. It was so simple—yet life changing. Supernatural healings began to happen after simple prayers were said over the sick people. Good news travels fast, and soon I had a house full of just ordinary people who were experiencing extraordinary things through God's Holy Spirit.

Over the years we have learned many things by trial and error. It became very clear to us that the only safe way to experience the supernatural presence and power of God was to base everything we experienced and taught squarely on the Word of God. We began saying about ourselves, "We are radical, but we are not weird."

Jesus preached a radical message and did radical things, but He was not weird. The Father authenticated His Son's identity by signs and wonders. The early believers' ministries were authenticated by the same supernatural signs of people being healed and set free from demonic bondages. It is the same today.

DEACON PHILIP IN SAMARIA

Acts 8 records the great persecution that arose against the Jerusalem church, scattering all except the apostles throughout the regions of Judea and Samaria. So dispersed, these believers preached the Word everywhere they went.

Deacon Philip "went down to the city of Samaria and preached Christ to them. And the multitudes with one accord heeded the things spoken by Philip, hearing and seeing the miracles which he did. For unclean spirits, crying with a loud voice, came out of many who were possessed; and many who were paralyzed and lame were healed. And there was great joy in that city" (Acts 8:5–8).

Jesus mentored the apostles, and taught and mentored the seventy, sending them out in His name. The apostles undoubtedly mentored the deacons, who were chosen to assume some of their responsibilities so they could study the Word and spend more time in prayer. Later, we see Paul mentoring others, and because of those relationships, we have the rich heritage of the letters he wrote to Timothy and Titus, his sons in the faith.

A CURIOUS BELIEVER

When Debbie visited our home group, she described herself as a curious evangelical believer who had heard about some of the exciting things happening at our meetings. Little did she know that she was going to encounter the Holy Spirit of God in a life-transforming way!

One evening at home group, John had a word of knowledge that someone with terrible allergies was going to be healed that very night. Debbie immediately spoke up. "I hope that's me you're talking about," she said, "because I have such terrible allergies that my medical records file is a foot thick." She went on to explain that she constantly used an inhaler and couldn't even wear eye makeup.

As we prayed with great faith and confidence because of the word of knowledge, she was healed. The next week Debbie had a story to tell about what the Lord had done for her. "Look, look, I even have eye makeup on!" she exclaimed. "And I don't even know where my inhaler is—maybe in a drawer at home— I haven't needed it!"

When someone experiences dramatic healing such as this, great faith for healing rises up in their heart. We began to encourage Debbie to pray for healing for others, and God answered her prayers. Enrolling in MTC, she got her theology sorted out and became a strong practicum group leader.

After Debbie graduated, our high school pastor asked her to consider starting some teenage small groups. Debbie went on to birth and coach twenty such groups! All of these changes took place in Debbie's life within a period of fourteen months. She is a second-generation leader of a Holy Spirit empowered small group who will soon head up a small group conference and raise up our third-generation leaders!

Does that excite you like it does us? Debbie's unquestionable anointing for ministry did not grow out of some structured leadership development program; it simply took place as a result of the Holy Spirit empowered organic growth cycle we have been explaining. It "just happens" if we invite the Holy Spirit to have His way in our midst.

Now we are seeing fruit from third-generation ministry. Just this week we learned of a sixteen-year-old high-schooler who is being used by God to pray for people in the marketplace, just as Debbie has trained her. Recently, this teenager was in a local business and was impressed to ask a certain young mother if she needed prayer. She discovered that the woman was overwhelmed and in a desperate state. Debbie's young disciple prayed with her, and the woman was deeply moved. She could hardly believe that God cared enough about her to have someone she didn't even know talk with her and pray for her.

The sixteen-year-old said she went in the women's restroom afterwards and bawled like a baby to think the Lord could use her this way.

Debbie is a wife and mother of three sons. She went from being a powerless, ineffective Christian to a powerhouse leader in a little over a year. If we are going to care for God's people, we need to provide a pathway to leadership for the Debbies of the world...and there are many more of them than you might imagine!

SURFACING THE GIFT

When Charles attended our home group, we saw the prophetic gift begin to surface in his life. When our church did *Forty Days of Purpose*, the fellow from our small group started a group in his own home for the forty days, and it flourished. Modeled after what Charles had experienced in our home group, they have Spirit-filled worship and personal prayer ministry as integral parts of their weekly meetings.

As a small group, they are "doing life together" in ever-increasing and meaningful ways. After completing *Forty Days of Purpose*, they went through our church's discipleship classes as a group. These are held on Sunday mornings during one of our three celebration services. This was in addition to their Monday evening small group gathering.

On Saturday mornings, this same team of people serve our community as part of Westside Church's "Adopt-A-Block" program, where we care for the less fortunate people in our community. This small group loves God and people. They spend five hours a week together (one hour class on Sunday, two hours on Monday evening, and two hours on Saturday serving the community).

Just think how much time so many of us waste watching worthless and often depressing television programs. This little band of brothers and sisters has chosen "the better way" of love and service. As a result, they are growing in Christ and live in a loving and safe environment for themselves and their children.

To our delight, we recently learned that this same small group plans to join our MTC in the fall—together! When they graduate the following May, we will have even more leaders ready to begin more small groups—that will likely follow the same pattern with the same results.

Allow me to repeat myself here. None of this developed as a result of some formalized "leadership development" program. It simply happened because we were willing to honor the Holy Spirit's presence at our small group gatherings. Yes, word certainly gets around, and the hopeless, hurting, and lost find their way to our home groups through loving family and friends. Once there, the ministry of the group in the power of the Holy Spirit changes their lives in such dramatic ways that they in turn tell others, and the cycle continues.

We believe with all our hearts that this Holy Spirit-perpetuated organic growth is the answer to lifeless, ineffective religion. It is making a strong difference in the health and life of our church. Pastor Ken says: "In a healthy human body, oxygen-rich cells carry life to every other cell in the corpus. If those blood cells lose their ability to deliver oxygen, fight infection, and carry away pollution, the entire body begins to break down. Healthy bodies are comprised of healthy, oxygen-rich cells. The Holy Spirit is the life-giving oxygen of the body of Christ. Spirit-filled small groups—cells like the Deckers's and the others launched from their group—are healthy blood cells that bring life to the entire church.

"Every single area of our body life, our community anatomy, has received healthy, life-building investment from these Spirit-saturated small groups. It would be virtually impossible to overstate the benefits of these groups at Westside Church."

Conservatively speaking, there are now several hundred Westsiders who are moving in this Holy Spirit-empowered ministry.

Bob and Judy

Bob and Judy moved to Bend and began looking for a church. Their grandson had been a student at Central Oregon Community College in Bend, and had attended Westside. He suggested they try it out.

Happily, there was no need of further "church shopping" after their first visit. Bob and Judy were ready to settle in and get involved. Before too long, they found their way to our home group, since they lived out in the area where we are located. Let's read about their experience in Judy's own words:

New to Central Oregon and looking for fellowship and accountability, little did we know how God would teach and care for us when we visited the Deckers' small group. Our evangelical and conservative church upbringings didn't teach the fullness of the Spirit of God. I'd had many spiritual experiences that I shared with willing listeners. However, I did not have an understanding or scriptural basis for these experiences. Needless to say, we were intrigued when we saw people being healed by simple prayers within the group. I was healed of fibromyalgia![1]

Our faith grew week after week as we saw the marvelous ways hurting and sick people were helped and healed. We, too, prayed and began to see our confidence grow.

John and Sonja always talk about beginning more small groups, and they asked us to let them know when we would be able to birth one! When our new home was finished, we did begin the group, and it has been a joy! We, like the Deckers, always have prayer ministry as a part of our group. One of our first group studies was Rick Warren's bestseller, *The Purpose Driven Life*. God has blessed us with a committed core group. We have had many answers to prayer.

Bob and I continue to attend the Deckers' group for our personal mentoring and growth. It is awesome to see new people to the group beginning to understand the power of prophetic prayer ministry, just like we did in the beginning.

And so the process continues. It has been so much fun to watch Bob and Judy progress from excited bewilderment to strong leaders who move in the power of the Holy Spirit. They, too, regularly experience supernatural healings in their small group.

Just this month they birthed another small group out of theirs, and we have asked them to become coaches over four small groups. That is more third-generation growth, and we are confident it will keep happening. What could possibly compare with the joyful fulfillment of watching men and women blossom and grow in Christ?

UNDER SPIRITUAL AUTHORITY

Training leaders to lead by the power of the Holy Spirit prevents any excesses or nonsense from being tolerated in our small groups. For example, one evening someone brought a guest to our home group. She was an extremely talkative and outgoing person and seemed quite opinionated.

We have a high tolerance for different personalities, and being gracious and grace-filled are hallmarks of our group. But there are limits. When the prayer ministry time came, instead of waiting for my direction as our group normally does, this woman jumped up and knelt before the woman who had been requesting prayer.

Now it so happened that John was out of the country on a missions trip, so I quickly moved to take authority when the woman began exhibiting some very disturbing physical and vocal expressions. I stood behind her, put my hand on her shoulder and quietly said, "We are not going there." She ignored me, and I squeezed her shoulder and said more loudly, "We are not going there—you are out of order."

"I can't help myself when the Holy Spirit comes upon me that way!" she exclaimed. "That's not even scriptural!" I replied. "Get up and sit in your chair." By then the tightened grip of my hand on her shoulder was non-verbally communicating, "Sister, you are not going any further!"

Reluctantly, she got up, sat down in her chair, and the group released a collective sigh of relief. I was still trying to discern if I was dealing with a demonic spirit or just an untaught, unsubmitted disciple. I asked two other people to minister to the woman who had initially requested prayer, and our meeting unfolded peacefully from there.

After the meeting the disruptive woman came and apologized for her behavior. She admitted that she didn't have to engage in those sorts of actions and expressions when she thought she sensed the Holy Spirit. I told her I accepted her apology, and then asked her if she was aware of the way our group had reacted to her out-of-order behavior. She nodded an affirmative, and admitted that was often the case when she prayed. I told her I had been prepared to ask her not to come again to the home group, but since she had apologized and seemed willing now to submit to the leader's authority, she was still welcome. She is not a regular member of the group, but occasionally attends if she needs prayer.

After she left, one of the women I am mentoring rushed to me and expressed her gratitude for the way I handled the situation. Apparently the woman had been at a prayer meeting the day before and had dominated and destroyed the usual peace and unity of that group. My friend said no one seemed to know what to do. She then asked me what she should do if such a circumstance arose again.

I reminded her of the necessity of always being under spiritual authority in such matters. If she was not leading such a meeting and discerned an inappropriate behavior, she should quietly go to the person in charge and voice her concerns. If the leader opted not to take action, she should then pray the Lord's protection for the group, and discuss it more fully with the leader afterwards.

My young disciple was thrilled to see how an uncomfortable situation and a difficult person could be graciously handled, while making sure the group was safe from people with their own agendas. In all the years of participation in small groups, we have found such situations to be extremely rare. So don't allow such a possibility to deter you from forming a Spirit-led group.

This example illustrates how a small group structure of leaders and coaches is imperative for healthy Holy Spirit empowered small groups. If leaders find themselves with a situation they have not dealt with before, they can always make a quick call to their coaches.

Literally hundreds of people have been in our home groups over the years. We have also witnessed multitudes of healings and deliverances. That is why our Christianity has never become dead religion—we make sure we are constantly in a faith-filled atmosphere where people are "doing the stuff" of ministry. Yes, it is still happening today, and it is always accompanied by great joy.

In the next chapter we will look at some of the "nuts and bolts" of the type of home group we are discussing.

Chapter 3

Small Group Anatomy

L EADERS OF THE type of groups we have been describing on these pages need to be filled with God's Spirit, and experienced enough to appropriately model the supernatural gifts of the Spirit. The gifts that are especially helpful in this type of ministry are words of wisdom and knowledge, discerning of spirits, and faith.[1]

Unlike gatherings that do a structured Bible study or discuss the pastor's Sunday sermon, these groups are utterly dependent upon the Holy Spirit for His life-giving presence. The leaders, therefore, must be willing to seek the Lord week by week for a direction, emphasis, or a short teaching for the gathering. Our experience bears out the fact that the Holy Spirit is always gracious to prepare and lead us if we ask Him what He would like to do that evening. Sometimes groups will choose to use a book with a study group application as a part of their gatherings, but ministry by the power of the Holy Spirit is always the chief emphasis.

A REPRODUCIBLE FORMAT

The following small group format has evolved over years of trial and error. It has not only worked well for us, it has also proven to be highly reproducible.

Frequency and time

The meeting is once a week (we chose Tuesday) from 7:00 pm to 9:00 pm. We meet year-round and have two couples that lead the meeting at our home if we are out of town. Continuity is a key factor for success.

Begin with refreshments

We always provide sweets, veggies, coffee, and tea. This is a good time for socializing and connecting on a personal level, and the segment lasts about fifteen minutes.

Leaders set the direction

Group leaders have sought the Lord for specific direction.

Worship

We begin with a short time of worship, seeking to teach the group how to allow the Holy Spirit to lead us in singing spiritual, unpremeditated songs of praise and adoration. Often the worship leader is a guitarist who enjoys leading this form of worship. This may be a new experience for guests. If it is, we explain from 1 Corinthians 14 exactly what we are going to do. We invite them to participate at their own comfort level. Some simply close their eyes and enjoy the unique and special presence of the Holy Spirit in this form of worship. It is sweet, and we experience a palpable sense of the Lord Jesus Christ in our midst. This praise and worship lasts about ten minutes and sets the stage for the next part of the gathering.

Introductions

If we have first-time guests (which we do almost every week), we each introduce ourselves. This is a way to get each attendee to participate. Following are some of the ice-breaker questions we use:

1. Let's introduce ourselves by telling where you attend church and how long you have lived in the area.

2. Quickly tell when and how you accepted the Lord Jesus Christ as your Savior (if you have). If you are still exploring the possibilities, you can say that.

3. Tell about a time when you thought you heard the voice of the Lord.

4. Share the circumstances surrounding your baptism in the Holy Spirit (if you have experienced that). If you are still exploring that significant step, tell us about it.

5. Tell what you are prepared to share with the group tonight. (It may be encouragement, mercy, faith for healing, a scripture, or a song.)

These introductions should take about twenty minutes. The leader is responsible to graciously remind the participants to be brief.

Biblical insights

Ask if anyone has a scripture or some insight they have received. (Sometimes groups will choose to use this time for a group discussion about a book they are reading, or perhaps the pastor's weekend message.) As people share, the leaders direct the conversation, keeping it Christ-centered and always ultimately edifying. Leaders must provide strong leadership for this part of the meeting. By providing a safe place where people can begin to participate in this type of ministry, there will be occasions when a short teaching is appropriate if someone is not quite on target with what they have shared. When done in a loving and scriptural way, all are instructed and built up. Again, this will usually take about thirty minutes.

MINISTRY TIME

Solicit answers to prayers and praise reports

This is when the gathering gets exciting! Week after week we see encouraging, faith-strengthening answers to our prayers from previous weeks. People can hardly wait to give honor and thanks to the Lord Jesus for what He has done. Faith begins to be released as people hear how God has saved, healed, delivered, restored relationships, or provided employment.

Solicit requests for prayer

People learn to give succinct statements and express exactly what they are believing God to do for them, so those praying can be in agreement.

Pray for the needs

Once prayer requests have been shared, the leaders need to be very sensitive to the Holy Spirit's leading in how, when, and who is to pray and minister to the expressed needs. We direct certain people to pray, usually teaming a more experienced person with the less experienced. We might say to them, "Remember to directly address the pain and command it to leave in the name of the Lord Jesus Christ." Make your prayers succinct. After they have prayed, we have them ask the person, "What is happening?" not "How do you feel?" Sometimes the person may say, "The pain isn't quite as bad, but not completely gone." We then tell them to pray once again and command the pain to completely leave and not return. They pray and ask once again what is happening, and more often than not, the pain is completely gone! Total ministry time takes about forty-five minutes.

Always, always, end on time. Again, leaders must stay in control of the meeting. The ministry is often so life-giving and exciting that people just don't want to stop. When people are instantly healed of some excruciating pain or migraine headache, there is a natural tendency to want to keep sharing, praying, and thanking the Lord Jesus for His awesome grace and power. Be that as it may, by teaching the group that it is imperative to start and stop on time, they understand why we draw things together at exactly 9:00 pm. Those who need to get home and to bed so they can rise at 5:00 am appreciate our commitment and respect for their schedule. If they stay until 11:00 pm, they may enjoy the moment, but the next morning they will have to drag themselves out of bed, be cross with their children, and not as productive at their place of employment. Therefore, the overall effect becomes negative.

CHILDREN AND SMALL GROUPS

Small group leaders need to give thoughtful prayer and attention to the needs of the children whose parents attend the group. Parents might want to consider arranging for child care in their home, so the children can be put to bed at appropriate times and so the parents can fully engage in the home group themselves. One of the greatest gifts parents can give to their children is to be in a weekly environment where they are giving and receiving ministry through the power of the Holy Spirit.

There are groups, of course, that want their children to be with them on home group evenings. If that is the case, we have found it works best if the host of the meeting has children, too. Some people choose to have the children be a part of the meeting until the worship time is completed. Others find it best to have them go directly to the room where they will be meeting. If at all possible, it usually works best to hire a babysitter, however, some parents choose to rotate being with the children.

The parents can decide if they want the evening to be a fun play time, a story time, or actually use an appropriate curriculum for the children. Snacks are very important, and the parent(s) who are to be with the children that particular evening usually bring them.

As we said, each group dynamic is different, and the responsibility is on the leaders/hosts to find what works best for the people attending.

PRE-CHRISTIANS WITNESS THE POWER OF GOD

Healing is a marvelous way to introduce people to the living Christ. Just recently, I stopped on the road in front of our five acres and engaged our neighbor, Fred, in conversation. He is a delightful man and a wonderful neighbor and friend. I asked him if he had been skiing. He explained he had hurt his back and couldn't get relief from the pain. I immediately invited him to our home group that evening, so we could pray for him and see what the Lord would do. Fred said he would like to do that, and we agreed he would come about 8:30 p.m. for prayer.

While he and his wife are not Christians, they have expressed their belief in the power of prayer. At exactly 8:30 p.m., Fred and Linda arrived. After he explained about his condition, the group prayed, and he felt some relief. By the next day or so he was completely healed. Our neighbor was extremely grateful and kept thanking the group and us. With a smile, I reminded Fred that we did not heal him—it was the Lord Jesus Christ.

This type of Christianity is authentic and powerful. Without putting expectations or pressure on our friends to become believers, we simply live out the New Testament model as accurately as we possibly can. In other words, we give them the opportunity to see the real deal.

This type of dynamic Holy Spirit empowered ministry inspires people to invite family, friends, neighbors, and coworkers for prayer and ministry. Some are Christians, some are not. It doesn't matter to us; we simply view them all as precious people whom God loves and desires to touch in ways that make Him real and relevant.

Because of the constant ebb and flow of visitors who become regular attendees, we are always thinking and talking about beginning new groups so that more people can be included. In the six years since we began our group, a dozen similar groups have launched. And guess what? These new groups are every bit as effective as ours, because it isn't John and Sonja doing the ministry, it is the group, and that is reproducible.

FIFTY BY SUMMER'S END

Last summer we decided not to begin new groups, reasoning that people would be on vacation and taking advantage of our Central Oregon high-desert weather and the multiple recreation opportunities. Our anticipated drop-off in attendance, however, never happened. In fact, we kept right on growing. By summer's end, over fifty people were showing up at our home group.

Thankfully, we are blessed with a large and very open house plan that allows us to accommodate such a group. A number that large under one roof is a bit of a challenge—and certainly a different dynamic. But it is also fun!

In the fall, we multiplied again into more groups of eight to ten people.

You can tell by now that one essential element for a Holy Spirit empowered small group is a constant flow of guests and new people joining in. As a result, no two meetings are exactly alike. The mix of people and the needs they have determine how the Holy Spirit will lead the meeting that particular evening.

That's the real beauty of this format. It encourages the possibilities of new people, different needs, and new opportunities for the Holy Spirit to show His nearness and power in supernatural ways.

Don't you think that's how it must have been in Jesus' ministry? The Lord and His disciples were constantly ministering to different people in very diverse conditions. Yes, it could have been rather hectic at times, but think how exciting it would have been to be there!

We have noticed that if there are no new guests, the meeting can quickly become predictable, lifeless, and lacking the spontaneity of the Holy Spirit.

BRIDGE TO HOPE

I serve on the board of directors of a ministry called Bridge to Hope. We help women inmates successfully transition from prison to meaningful and productive lives. It was founded by Linda Swearingen, a human dynamo and a great friend of ours. She is, by admission, a "recovering politician" (former mayor, county commissioner, and lobbyist).

The ministry's success rate is phenomenal. So much so, that the Department of Labor regularly invites Linda to speak at their regional conferences to explain how the program works. Linda attended our first MTC here at the Bend church, and it changed her in marvelous ways—especially in the small group practicum sessions. Here's her story:

> Five years ago, a friend invited me to take MTC training with her at Westside Church. In the beginning I wasn't sure whether I wanted to commit nine months of my life to a Bible training program. I had grown up in a Christian home, attended Sunday school, church camp, and other Bible training sessions over the years, and I felt that I had a good grasp of the Word of God. However, I didn't know how to apply the Word to my life until I participated in MTC.
>
> Prior to attending the training, I had very little personal experience "doing what Jesus did." I had read about miracles, and, from time to time, I had even witnessed supernatural events from a distance, but up-close-and-personal miracles were a rare event in my life.
>
> Six months before I attended the first MTC meeting, I had rededicated my life to Jesus. I had come to a point where I no longer wanted just a "death benefit policy" with my Lord and Savior, but I wanted a close personal

relationship with Him. Soon after I had made the decision to have a deeper walk with God, I began to work with female ex-felons and drug addicts as they transitioned from jail and prison back into society.

My experience with women in recovery and my career as a local politician often led me to my knees. I knew in my heart that Jesus was the answer, but at times I felt so unprepared to deal with life's challenges. After hearing about MTC, I thought I would attend a few sessions just to see if it was going to be helpful in my situation. The very first night we were introduced to personal ministry. Within weeks, we were expected to lead pre-Christians to the Savior, heal the sick, and set the captives free.

At first I was a little skeptical that all of us "ordinary folks" would be carrying out the Great Commission. I had always figured that the local preacher, the traveling evangelists, and missionaries were given the responsibility of performing miracles. Our job was to get the unsaved, the sick, and those in need of deliverance to church, and God would meet their needs there. I never really expected to see miracles up close and personal for myself.

One evening at MTC, John Decker anointed our hands with oil and prayed that God would use us to heal the sick. He also prayed that God would bring those in need of healing directly to us. Within days of John's prayer and directive for us to go and heal the sick, a number of people I came in contact with were in desperate need of healing. They were high-level politicians, including a governor, and a rag-tag little old man alongside the road with a sign saying that he needed a ride to our local hospital.

One of the female ex-felons was with me in the car and wanted me to pick up the little old man with the sign. I told her I didn't pick up hitchhikers, but she insisted, so I turned around and picked him up. He poured out a heartbreaking story of his wife dying and then his being in a horrible car accident and that he was in excruciating pain. He could not drive to the hospital. I asked him if I could pray for him, and he practically jumped into the front seat with us. I prayed for healing and that he would personally come to know Jesus as Lord. He was profusely thanking me as he exited the car.

If you pray, you will get opportunities!

Linda has brought many of the women from her ministry to our home group, where they are warmly greeted and accepted. This is part of their "bridge to hope" experience, where they see ordinary Christians loving, respecting, and helping each other on the journey to health and wholeness.

The Cycle Continues

It's inevitable that people attending home groups, experiencing the type of ministry we have been describing, soon inquire about receiving more training. When enthusiastic MTC grads and current students explain how they have personally benefited from the MTC, it is always compelling. Year after year as September rolls around, large groups of eager students are ready to enroll.[2] And so the cycle continues:

- Personal experience at a home group

- Desire for more training

- Enroll in a Ministry Training Center

- Graduate

- Begin a Holy Spirit empowered home group and/or enter service/ministry/leadership roles in the local church or para-church organizations

- Become an effective marketplace Christian.

All of this significant activity finds its genesis in the Holy Spirit and His gifts. In the next chapter we will explore how His gifts heal, build up, and strengthen each individual believer, thereby strengthening the whole church.

Chapter 4

Releasing Gifts of the Holy Spirit

JESUS TOLD HIS disciples that He was going away to prepare a place for them where they would be with Him at a future time. Then He commanded them to wait in Jerusalem for the promised gift of power from His heavenly Father. This coming One, He explained, would be their Teacher, Counselor, and Comforter. He would be the one who would empower them to fulfill His very last instructions—the Great Commission to go into all the world.

And being assembled together with them, He commanded them not to depart from Jerusalem, but to wait for the promise of the Father:

> "Which," He said, "you have heard from Me; for John truly baptized with water, but you shall be baptized with the Holy Spirit not many days from now." Therefore, when they had come together, they asked Him, saying, "Lord, will You at this time restore the kingdom to Israel?" And He said to them, "It is not for you to know times or seasons which the Father has put in His own authority. But you shall receive power when

the Holy Spirit has come upon you; and you shall be witnesses to Me in Jerusalem, and in all Judea and Samaria, and to the end of the earth."

—Acts 1:4–8

These things I have spoken to you while being present with you. But the Helper, the Holy Spirit, whom the Father will send in My name, He will teach you all things, and bring to your remembrance all things that I said to you.

—John 14:25–26

The Arrival

The Book of Acts church was birthed on the Day of Pentecost—just a few short days after the Lord Jesus gave the Great Commission.

The Holy Spirit came in a mighty rush of supernatural power. He came upon Peter, enabling the impulsive, rough-edged fisherman to speak with such clarity and anointing that three thousand Jews gave their hearts to the Lord Jesus Christ that day!

And here we are, over two thousand years later, and the Holy Spirit is still coming upon people and empowering them to fulfill the Great Commission in their generation.

This gift from our Father in Heaven is of inestimable value, as was the gift of His Son. In each case, it meant God Himself breaking into His own fallen creation, so He could have an up-close relationship with us. What a staggering thought!

The Holy Spirit is the heavenly gift-giver. He is instrumental in our salvation because He draws us to God. As we repent from our life of sin and separation from God, inviting the Lord Jesus to come into our lives, the Spirit comes and indwells us, bringing the gifts He desires to give to others through us. He does all the "hard stuff."

Our part is to be obedient and surrender to His leading. That should be the "easy stuff," but with our fallen nature always trying to elbow its way in and exert itself, it isn't so easy.

When we speak of "releasing gifts of the Holy Spirit," we envision layers of gifting....

- The Holy Spirit Himself comes to us as *the* gift from heaven.

- Filling us up with Himself, He gives us supernatural gifts.

- We begin to exercise other gifts and talents from the Holy Spirit.

- As individual believers, *we* are gifts within the church.

The Gift From Heaven

On the day of Pentecost, the Promised One arrived with astounding results. He, the Holy Spirit, has beautiful gifts to give to God's sons and daughters. Some are supernatural; others are talents and unique abilities.

The Holy Spirit is the one who determines and decides how His life-giving and edifying gifts will be distributed within God's family. We regularly see the following supernatural gifts in our gatherings:

- words of wisdom
- words of knowledge
- miracles (in the form of instant healings)
- faith
- prophecy
- tongues
- interpretation of tongues
- discerning of spirits
- deliverance/exorcism

Again, in the context of our small groups, we also see the expression of other gifts and talents:

- evangelism
- administration
- craftsmanship
- intercession
- giving
- helps/service
- hospitality
- creativity gifts
- counseling
- encouragement
- leadership
- mercy
- shepherding (pastor)
- teaching

"You are such a gift to me," is a fairly common phrase. When we say that, we are usually expressing our gratitude and thankfulness for someone's kindness, encouragement, or other pleasing actions. The church of the living God is made up of individual Christians who are to be good gifts to one another, as well as to pre-Christians.

UNTAPPED RESOURCES

As we contemplated and prayed about how we as the church could embrace what the Holy Spirit wants to do, it occurred to us that there are several vast untapped resources that are sitting in our churches.

Charismatic Christians

The first group consists of hundreds of thousands of Christians who experienced the great charismatic renewal of the sixties and seventies. Millions of Christians worldwide experienced being baptized in the Holy Spirit, and began praying in languages they had not learned. Many of them were also empowered with supernatural gifts of healing and prophecy.

The following excerpt from a student's final exam at the

North Coast Bible Institute in Eureka, California is typical of the Christians we are discussing:

> When I first became a Christian in 1972, it was very natural for me to lay hands on those in our prayer group and pray for healing. Almost every time we prayed, the healing prayed for was accomplished either instantly or within a few days. Those were exciting times. Shortly thereafter we moved, and while attending a Spirit-filled church, our small groups focused on "studies," rather than just the Word and ministering to one another in Christ.
>
> Over the intervening years I have grown a little deaf about the promptings of the Holy Spirit to pray for healing for others and myself. I rather expect that the gifts of healings will once again be manifested through me, as we will be leading a small home group starting in February.

These Christians need to be identified, awakened, retooled, and mobilized for the end-time harvest we are anticipating. This student clearly articulates our premise that home groups must have the element of "ministering to one another in Christ," or face the possibility of becoming stagnant, with very little life-changing activity.

Now please don't get us wrong. We highly value Bible study. God's Word is the basis for all we seek to accomplish in our ministry and in our lives. But to just have study without the life-giving ministry of the Holy Spirit flowing through the participants tends to make the group more ingrown—perhaps even "academic" at times. Such a focus on "Bible only" rarely produces an atmosphere conducive to inviting coworkers, friends, neighbors, and relatives, so they can experience salvation, Holy Spirit baptism, healing, and even deliverance on occasion.

We have had many, many people visit our group, who at one time in their lives had participated in the exhilarating experience of praying for one another in the Spirit. At the end of the meeting they are exuberant, describing the evening like a drink of refreshing cool water to their parched souls. Yes, these thirsty folks are out there in our congregations. We need to find them and get them ready for the challenging days ahead.

The Jesus People

This is yet another group that spontaneously emerged in the late sixties. They, too, experienced the supernatural power of God that set them free from drugs, healed them of nightmare flashbacks, and gave their lives meaning and purpose. Many of the ones we know are still somewhat radical in their Christianity—that's just who they are, and they have a unique ability to relate to our youth better than most adults. One brother still has a highly effective skateboard ministry with the youth. Let's also identify these men and women who experienced such a dramatic deliverance from a culture of drugs and "free love," and include them in our efforts to reach the next major group, our youth.

Youth

During the last several years, the Lord has led us to once again work with youth. Wow! What an energizing experience! Their music may be loud, but the message shines out brightly. The other thing we have discovered is their desperate hunger for the reality of the supernatural power of God.

Let's face it, Americans have become fascinated with the supernatural. Just look at the bestselling books, box office hits, and some of the most watched television programs. Interest in the occult seems to be flourishing wherever you turn. Even young children can check out witchcraft or sorcery how-to books from public libraries.

We, as human beings, crave to explore that which we intuitively know to be an integral part of our lives—the supernatural. And who has more to say on that issue than the mighty Spirit of God Himself, who indwells, fills, and overflows His people? Unfortunately, the church has mostly quelled the supernatural activity of the Holy Spirit through the years.

Aren't you glad our God has never given up on us? Across the centuries He has continued to reveal Himself to open and willing hearts. The resultant awakenings, revivals, renewals, and powerful moves of God have kept the church alive, giving testimony to a dark and dying world. Now it's our time, our opportunity to hear and obey His call to prepare for the harvest.

RISE OUT OF SLUMBER

We older ones who have previously experienced the ministry of the Holy Spirit need to arise out of our slumber and help these young men and women to find the realities they so fervently seek.

Returning and retired missionaries are another excellent group of individuals who often have worlds of practical experience to share with less-seasoned believers.

As we mentioned previously, we have nineteen-year-olds in our MTCs this year who minister with power through the Holy Spirit. They prophesy, heal the sick, correctly discern spiritual activity, and are fearless in the face of the enemy!

We have committed ourselves to do everything we can to identify, train, mentor, and release these young people into the crucial, groundbreaking ministries preordained for them by the Lord Jesus.

The next chapter demonstrates the commonality of believers from diverse age groups and backgrounds who love and care for each other in the warm, secure environment of a Holy Spirit empowered small group.

Chapter 5

What Do They Have in Common?

WHAT DO 747 pilots, loggers, homemakers, physicians, and college students have in common? What could possibly draw together such diverse people with entirely different educational, cultural, and economic backgrounds?

It's not a "what." It's a "Who." The Holy Spirit of God Almighty.

As spiritual beings, we humans were designed with an intense desire to understand and experience the supernatural touch of God on our lives. Christians long for the "something more" they intuitively know must exist. Given such a strong, innate desire, when people hear about a home group where men and women are being healed and even set free from destructive, addictive habits, they want to "come and see."

Many believers who aren't drawn at all to structured book or Bible studies may become curious about a group where the supernatural takes place. They may very well give such a group a try.

Our responsibility as leaders is to provide a safe environment where the curious, the hurting, and the seekers can be introduced to a living, powerful God. We have previously outlined the way the process seems to work best by Holy Spirit empowered organic growth as opposed to a tightly structured program. Now we will look at the loving community that can exist when the Holy Spirit is in charge.

Erasing Generational Barriers

We have people of all ages who have been a part of our home groups over the years. When given an opportunity, youngsters, teens, moms and dads, singles, and grandmothers and grandfathers are knit together. This dynamic applies both to our home groups and our MTCs. (This year's MTC at our home church has a nineteen-year-old and an eighty-six-year-old—and they're both loving it!)

Just last Monday night at our MTC, I greeted Corey, one of our Cascade Master Commission (CMC) students. "Hey, Miss Sonja," he smiled. "It's good to see you!" I then inquired about their weekend gig in Albuquerque.

Corey and his brother Casey, along with a couple of other guys, all in their twenties, have an excellent worship band. They are true worshipers, not entertainers, and we love these young men. They have destiny written all over them, as does their other brother Jason. (I often say to our CMC interns, "When I look into your eyes, I see my future, and it's exciting!")

Corey could hardly wait to describe what it was like to get a taste of what he wants to do for the rest of his life. My heart brimmed over with God's love for this gifted, humble young man as he explained that the band had not only led worship for the hundreds of teenagers at the conference, but they preached, taught breakout sessions, and had rap sessions with the kids. Beyond a doubt, he knew they had left a life-changing deposit in that city. He said he wanted to always have at least two days at these meetings, so that the team could spend quality time with the kids, and truly invest in their lives.

What a heart! As I walked away from that conversation, I felt such joy welling up in my spirit. Here John and I are, at our age, getting the opportunity to observe close-up what was happening in these young lives. I regularly remind them during prayer before worship that, "You are the anointed of the Lord." And they are!

Another relationship that brings me great joy and delight is with a seventeen-year-old who asked me to be her mentor. This blonde, blue-eyed beauty is a worship leader, keyboardist, singer, and songwriter named Whitney. Each time we meet, I come away amazed at the spiritual depth of this young woman.

We both know that her spiritual heritage has played a very significant role in who she is today. Her parents, Steve and Bo, are the pastors and leaders over the hundreds of young people at our church.

Whitney's godly family background and her strong commitment to Christ make her something of a conundrum to her coworkers at one of our local Starbucks. She is beautiful, seventeen, and never been kissed (because of living by her own standards, not because of a lack of interest from the young men)!

Her coworkers are amazed when they learn she has never smoked, drank, had sex, or been to wild parties. With a captivating smile, she simply tells them she has no need for those things. She goes on to explain what she does enjoy... things like leading worship for hundreds of teens each week and doing fun activities in groups where situations don't get out of control.

Lest I make her out to be perfect, I need to add that she is like all teens, learning how to have healthy relationships and boundaries, wanting to make wise decisions about her future career, and dreaming about the godly man she will one day marry—normal stuff. No, there are no generational barriers in this Spirit-led lifestyle.

ERASING CULTURAL AND ECONOMIC BARRIERS

During a class at our home church here in Bend, John was especially drawn to a man we had never met. After the class, he went over and introduced himself to the stranger. They visited for a few minutes, and then John invited him to our home group. He was a retired 747 pilot who was on an intense search for a meaningful relationship with the Lord Jesus Christ. His wife is a lovely woman and a devout Catholic, and we were thrilled when they attended our home group together.

Over the years we have become good friends, and have had the privilege of counseling and encouraging them through some tough times. They say their marriage is the healthiest it has ever been, and the home group played a significant role in their healing.

We share this to show how being obedient to a simple leading during a class could eventually result in a momentous life change for a struggling couple.

Most of the people who have attended our home groups over the years have been middle- to upper-class Americans. From time to time, however, someone invites a man or woman fresh out of prison or off the streets. We warmly welcome them all and do everything we can to make them comfortable in our gathering.

One night a woman who attends our group explained that she had met a man at a county office that had just been released from prison that day. Everything he owned, she told us, was in a small box under his arm. Learning that he only had the clothes on his back, she said she was sure she could help. He was to call the church the next day and ask for her.

We learned that the man was about John's size, and as soon as our home group was over that night, we went into our closet, and, beginning with underwear and socks, started putting together several outfits for this released prisoner—including shirts, pants, and shoes. We were heading for the coat closet to get a jacket when one of our first-time guests, a medical doctor, took off his brand new Columbia brand jacket and donated it to the worthy cause.

The man did call the church office the next day, received the clothes, and asked for John's telephone number. With tears of gratitude, he expressed how deeply it moved Him to think the Lord would take such good care of him. As the saying goes, that was an opportunity for us to be "Jesus with skin on."

When we become aware of a legitimate financial need in our midst, we usually can meet it through the open-hearted generosity of those in attendance. Sometimes it's a business owner, stepping up to provide employment for the distressed person. Frequently, it's simply a matter of people pulling out their checkbooks as the Lord moves their hearts.

Whether our guests are very wealthy or desperately poor, we as leaders try to treat every individual with the same measure of honor and respect. The wealthy appreciate not being fawned over, and those in difficult financial straits appreciate being treated like all the others. Somehow, we think Jesus would like this approach. And we're positive that the apostle James would! (See James 2:1–5.)

BUILDING WITHOUT FOUNDATIONS

It's not unusual for people to show up at our home group who have been Christians for many years, but are still "spiritual infants." Most of us realize that we can't judge maturity by the number of years since a person accepted Jesus Christ as his or her Savior. Without proper discipleship, people can make an initial step toward Christ but experience little, if any, growth through the years. That's one reason we begin our MTC curriculum with a lesson on repentance, conversion, salvation, and what we receive at the time of this experience.

When people begin to express their frustrations about not hearing God's voice or not being able to break free from long-standing habits, addictions, or bondages, our ears perk up. We immediately ask them to share with the group about their salvation experience. Often they haltingly describe raising their hand in response to an altar call for salvation, and expressing their desire at that moment for change in their lives. We carefully listen for any indication that they repented of their sins. When nothing is mentioned, we ask them if they understand that repenting and confessing of sins are part of the conversion process.

Sometimes, in response, we get blank, uncomprehending stares. At that point we open the Bible and explain how they can receive Jesus Christ as Lord and Savior, and find forgiveness from their sins. Many times these spiritually hungry individuals experience conversion right on the spot as we pray with them.

Prior to this conversation, if we asked them if they knew they would be with the Lord when they died, we might get a response like, "I don't know" or "I hope so" or maybe "Can a person really know for sure?"

After they understand and experience confession, repentance, and conversion, we ask the question again, and they confidently answer, "Yes!" We then immediately discuss with them the need for both water baptism and Holy Spirit baptism, and lead them into these powerful, supernatural experiences. As a result, these new believers receive the ability to pray perfect prayers according to the will of God in their Holy Spirit inspired prayer language.

No wonder they arrived at home group disillusioned about their life in Christ. They were trying to live the Christian life without an authentic conversion!

NEW TESTAMENT PATTERN

In the Book of Acts, the new converts were immediately baptized in water and in the Holy Spirit. We long to see a return to this New Testament pattern.

It is our opinion that much of the anemia and lukewarmness of today's Christian church can be attributed to this lack of foundation in millions of lives. It's almost as if they have been inoculated against a true, life-changing encounter with the risen Christ. Let's provide safe home groups where they can learn what the authentic born-again experience is all about.

So what do 747 pilots, loggers, homemakers, physicians, and college students have in common?—a life-changing, powerful encounter with the Holy Spirit of God in a small group.

So far we have mentioned several healings that have taken place in our home groups and as a result of the Ministry Training Center. The next chapter contains the stories of some of those who have been touched by the Healer.

Chapter 6

Healed and Set Free

W E MUST BE very careful to give God all the credit whenever people are healed or set free in any gathering; small or large. If we believe God to be the source of all healing, then we cannot ascribe *any part* of the miracle to how many people were praying, the way we prayed, or our style of ministry.

God does it all. The only part we can play is our willingness to obey what the Holy Spirit wants to do. Our part boils down to one word: obedience.

The likelihood of a healing taking place when we pray is greatly increased when the Holy Spirit Himself is directing the ministry. In fact, our experience confirms that in most cases of instant healings, they can be traced to a word of knowledge or a word of wisdom just prior to the touch of God. The small group is the best place to witness God moving in power to heal and deliver.

Many of us have convinced ourselves that miracles would most likely happen in big rallies, special meetings, or perhaps in some faraway third-world country. We have concluded that healings and deliverances happen wherever expectant Christians gather.

What do we mean by "expectant"? Simply that the leader of the gathering has created an expectation within the group, and is prepared to allow the Lord to reveal Himself in profound and spontaneous ways. What better way for Him to do that than in situations where everyone can witness a miracle?

We believe the small group is tailor-made for God to heal and set people free. Others in the group can marvel, learn by asking questions about what just happened, or simply praise God and rejoice for the ones healed.

It is less mystical and seems more authentic when it happens in the living room of a home among a small group of people. Everyone in the room knows it was God. The leader simply paved the way for the Holy Spirit to do what He does best, bring glory to Jesus Christ, and the group goes home with fresh understanding of how the Lord heals and truly desires to bless those who are simply obedient. And God receives all the glory and honor for confirming what He said He would do in the Word.

The result is that even more people show up the next week! The small group becomes not so small anymore, and plans begin for birthing the same kind of group across town.

HEALING ACCOUNTS

The following are actual accounts of people receiving positive physical changes in their bodies as a result of prayer in our small group. We have been careful to only include testimonies of those we know personally, and whose stories have been validated by medical professionals. Since these healings happen week after week, year after year, there are a multitude of testimonies we could have included. For the sake of space, however, we have selected a half dozen that are representative of the type of supernatural healings that are commonplace at our gatherings.

We always praise and thank the Lord in everything that happens, regardless of how small or insignificant the answer to prayer may be. We often ask the person who has just been healed, "Who did that? Who healed you?" They, of course, respond, "Jesus!" We never want them to focus on us as the people simply doing the praying. He receives all the glory.

Sharon's Story

In 1977, I was involved in a head-on vehicle collision that resulted in constant pain and chronic fatigue. It took several months before a diagnosis was reached. After visiting numerous doctors, I was diagnosed with fibromyalgia, and during the next five years, I tried many different procedures to find relief. Among the many therapies tried were the following: mega vitamin B shots, massage therapy, acupuncture, colonics, human growth hormone therapy, chiropractic, vitamin and herbal supplements (up to sixty tablets a day), magnetic therapy, osteopath, anti-depressants, sleeping meds (at least five different types), thyroid medication, detox programs, special diets, and special mattresses and pillows—all with little or no effects.

I was so weak that I had to choose one activity daily, and then spend the rest of the day resting. After five years of this, I was invited to John and Sonja Decker's home group to be prayed over. I had been prayed for in the past, but I had never experienced the power of prayer as I did with this group. I felt at ease as the group gathered around me, laying hands on me, and praying in different prayer languages.

After a few days passed, I began to feel a little stronger. The aches and pains were starting to subside. Within a month I began feeling much better. I gave up all other therapies and still improved. Now over two years have passed, and I feel like a new person. I owe my healing to God and to those faithful servants, John and Sonja and the others in their home group. I am extremely thankful to God for my healing, and I am very thankful that home groups exist where love and care are expressed for one another—where we can come together and pray and encourage one another and experience the power of God to heal, both physically and emotionally. Praise be to God!

John's Story

Eighty-six years old and full of life—that's how we describe our friend John. He and his wife Phyllis are regulars at our home group, loved by everyone who attends. John still cuts firewood and maintains their property better than many men his junior. John had accepted the Lord as a youngster, but walked away from Him for over seventy-five years. A few years back, he and Phyllis started attending church again. John reflected that there was still something missing—until he was invited to our small group.

Because he physically works so hard, he occasionally hurts or strains himself. Even so, John says that the hard work keeps him going. He has personally experienced healing of his shoulder, back, legs, and eyes. The Lord keeps renewing him and his strength.

One night last year, Phyllis asked if they could attend our MTC in the fall. We told them of course they were welcome, but that it was quite a commitment. They said they wanted to be trained to minister in the power of the Holy Spirit, and weren't concerned that it was once a week for nine months. The fact that they lived forty miles from the church in Bend also didn't deter them. Our winters in the high desert of central Oregon include lots of snow, ice, and winter storms, but again, John and Phyllis refused to be intimidated by such obstacles. They enrolled, have missed only two Monday nights, and will graduate this year.

John and Phyllis have learned how to share their faith, pray for the sick, recognize demonic activity, and were baptized in the Holy Spirit. Just last night, with a big smile on his face, John told the group about leading two people into the Holy Spirit baptism.

We suggested that perhaps they would want to skip our home group while attending the MTC, but they love it so much they never miss a Tuesday night meeting. In addition, they attend another small group that was birthed out of ours a couple of years ago. As a result of these commitments, their schedule shapes up like this: church on Sunday, MTC Monday night (roundtrip of eighty miles!), Deckers' home group Tuesday night, church again on Wednesday night, and the other small group on Friday night! We marvel at their stamina and joy in the Lord.

John says our home group is where they have truly experienced "church" by being loved, accepted, trained, and used.

Dave's Story

After watching people getting healed of various pains and physical conditions, first-time guest Dave B. requested healing of the chronic back pain he had suffered for over three years. He explained how he had been to many doctors and therapists, but none of them had given him relief. The group gathered around him, laid hands on where he was in pain, and spoke healing in the mighty name of Jesus Christ.

Dave noticed an immediate improvement, and in about thirty minutes, he came to John and exclaimed, "I am totally healed and pain free!" He was understandably excited and thankful for what Jesus had done. We left for a ministry trip the next day, and Dave spoke with our assistant. He poured out his gratitude for a small group where anyone could come and receive such life-changing, Holy Spirit empowered ministry. He was pain-free for the first time in over three years, and he was happy!

Kirk's Story

I was playing tag football on a church team on New Year's Day. It was very cold, and when I fell on my shoulder, I knew I had hurt it pretty bad. I went to the doctor and he diagnosed a partially torn rotator cuff, and recommended physical therapy.

After six weeks of therapy, I noticed little difference in the pain. Sleeping was very difficult, and I was severely restricted in physical activity. I belong to John and Sonja Decker's home group, and one night I asked for prayer for healing. The group gathered around me, laid hands on my shoulder, anointed me with oil in the name of the Lord Jesus Christ, and spoke healing to my shoulder.

I didn't feel a difference until I woke up the next morning and discovered how well I had slept—and that I didn't have a bit of pain! I was amazed! It has never bothered me again, and I play sports, including racquetball as often as I can. I know it was Jesus Christ who did the healing, but He used the wonderful people in my home group. I am very thankful to the Lord.

Judy K.'s Story

Judy and her husband Bob had moved to our area, attended our church, and looked for a small group. Since we lived in the same general area, they joined our group. They are both strong, winsome Christians and had always been in leadership in their church. Joining our group, however, they said they wanted to learn more about the Holy Spirit. The spontaneous healing taking place during the gatherings was all new to them. Little did they know the same blessing of physical wholeness awaited them, too!

I had never even thought of God's healing touch. I had suffered about ten years, done pain medication studies at Oregon State University Hospital, and even agreed to taking heavy-duty prescription drugs. After a hip replacement, I had been able to leave the prescription drugs, but really relied on over-the-counter meds.

In our small group, prayer for healing from pain was offered, and I immediately accepted that invitation. After prayer, the next three nights the pain really fired off so intensely that heat and over-the-counter meds didn't touch it. I felt embarrassed that healing hadn't happened, sensed that the evil one was doing a big number on my body, and I determined to only give God credit for what I knew He desired to do—heal my pain!

The second week at our small group prayer time, I shared my experience, named the evil one as responsible for lingering pain, declared my humility, and asked for prayer again for healing from fibromyalgia. God blessed! Praise the Lord! I have been free from pain from fibromyalgia for about three years at this writing. I really believe that God also worked with me mentally and emotionally, allowing me to understand that the fibromyalgia wasn't me, didn't belong within me, and could be denied residence in my body.

I had declared those things years before. However, I had not been in a Holy Spirit-led prayer meeting with spiritual warriors who laid hands on me and claimed the promises of Scripture. God just took it and destroyed all traces of residue in my body.

Tami's Story

Sometimes, during our ministry time, we discern a spirit of infirmity as the source of an individual's physical ailments and maladies. We take authority over the spirit in the mighty name of Jesus Christ, and they are set free and healed.

This spirit often plagues an individual with numerous physical ailments that physicians have trouble diagnosing. It seems to literally go from one part of the body to another, and it causes severe pain, discomfort, and depression until it is discerned and cast out.

Over a period of several years, I was having intermittent pains in different areas of my body. I had a sharp pain in my left foot. I had appointments with two doctors who found nothing wrong. I had sinus pressure and drainage. I had appointments with four doctors and had a CT scan, and they found nothing wrong. I also had pain in my right wrist and arm, so I had an appointment with a specialist for possible carpal tunnel, and he found nothing wrong.

My husband and I had heard about the Deckers' home group, and wanted to attend. We decided to go. That whole day I was attacked with pain and symptoms in all three areas. I contemplated not going, but we did.

While at the Deckers' home group, I asked for prayer for healing. I shared with the group what I had been experiencing. It was revealed that these symptoms were the result of a spirit of infirmity. I was prayed over. The prayers spoke directly to the spirit of infirmity. I felt my body slightly shaking, then the pain left my foot and my wrist, and the pressure in my sinus area was gone.

Occasionally one of these symptoms will try to start up again. I take authority in the name of Jesus, rebuke the spirit of infirmity, and it leaves. Praise God! I am healed!

Judi T.'s Story

We teach our students in the Ministry Training Centers and the people in our home group that healing is to be used in the marketplace. Again, if we are expectant and watching for opportunities, God is so gracious and loving that He will heal people we encounter outside our homes and churches. We call this marketplace ministry and cite a couple of examples below.

I was standing in my vet's office one day waiting to check in, and I heard the door start to open behind me. Not wanting my dog Bubba to jump up on the people, I wrapped my hand through his leash. Sure enough, he lunged, I felt something pop in my hand, and it started to burn and throb.

The next day I didn't know what I was going to do. We didn't have medical insurance and there was this huge red line going from my middle finger down the back of my hand, and I could barely open and close it.

My friend Sonja came into the salon where I work to get her hair done. She noticed that I was trying to stretch my hand, and she sweetly asked me if she could pray for me. I thought to myself, "What's to lose?" She took my hand and prayed. The first time it felt a little better, so she took it and prayed again, and the pain went away! By the next day the deep red line started to disappear. Sonja had told me to keep praying and thanking God for my healing. It took a couple of weeks, but my hand completely healed and works normally. Thank You, Lord!

HAIR SALON HEALINGS

Over the years I have had the privilege of helping my hairdressers come into relationship with the Lord Jesus Christ. A few months ago, I dropped John off to get his hair cut while I ran an errand. When I returned, his hairdresser was just finishing up, and turned to walk to the counter to process his credit card. As she began to walk, she was obviously in great pain—to the degree that she was dragging her leg and had her hand on her hip. I asked her what had happened, and she explained that she had hurt her hip and was in tremendous pain when she walked.

Jolene is a pre-Christian, and I was sure she didn't know anything about divine healing. Nevertheless, I felt prompted to say, "Jolene, you know the kinds of things we do, including praying for people. Would you allow us to pray for you?"

She looked at me with an incredulous expression. "Pray? Right here? Right now?"

"Yes," I answered, "and we won't embarrass you. But sometimes people are immediately healed as we pray."

"Well…okay," she replied.

I asked her to put her hand where the pain was. I then placed my hand over hers and simply spoke to the pain, rebuking it in the mighty name of the Lord Jesus Christ and commanding it to leave her body. She finished the credit card transaction, turned, and walked across the room to her station.

She then proclaimed very loudly, "You guys are freaking me out! My hip is not hurting! The pain is completely gone!" Now everyone in the salon was listening as she excitedly explained what had happened. It was awesome!

Recently, John was in for another haircut, and asked Jolene about her hip. "It's healed," she said, "completely and totally, and I've been telling everyone about it. By the way, you said you were going to bring me a copy of your book about this stuff." John apologized for forgetting to bring her a copy of *Doing What Jesus Did*, and assured her he would get it to her right away.

When he came home, he told me of his conversation with her. As it happened, I too was going to the salon later in the day for an appointment with my hairdresser, who works for Jolene.

"Great," he said. "I'll sign a book for her and you can take it."

Jolene was surprised to see me when I walked in the door, and was happy to receive the book. As I was turning to go upstairs where my hairdresser works, Jolene said, "Oh, Sonja, Susan needs to see you." (She is another beautiful pre-Christian who works in that same salon.)

As I opened the door upstairs, Susan was hanging up the telephone. "Sonja, Jolene just told me that I need to talk with you before you leave."

"Great," I answered. "I'll be happy to."

As it happened, Susan finished with her client before Judi was finished cutting my hair, so she came over and leaned against the wall next to me. I asked her what was wrong, and she explained that she had hurt her knee. It had been hyper-extended, so she had a brace on it, and it was extremely painful.

She began to question me, asking what I would do if I prayed for her. I explained that Jesus Christ loved her so much that He would like to reveal Himself to her, and that many times He heals when we pray in His name.

Susan then told me about an experience she'd had at a church where people prayed for her and "really got worked up and out of control." The experience had frightened her (as it would most anyone). I assured her I would not do that, and then she asked me if I could pray for her right then.

So get this picture: Judi was cutting my hair, and I reached out my hand to Susan's knee, rebuking the pain and speaking healing in Jesus' name. She began to bend her knee, stunned by the instant change. As she walked around the room, she exclaimed her gratitude. She said she could now bend her knee, but there was still a little pain.

Judi spoke up. "Susan, just have her pray a second time—that's what she did for my hand," and she proceeded to tell how she had been healed. So, I prayed again, and the pain left. Remember, two of these three hairdressers were not Christians; but they had been introduced to the Lord Jesus Christ through His goodness in healing them. What a gracious God we serve!

Every week someone in our small group or MTC has a testimony of ministering in the marketplace. These testimonies build the faith of the others, and soon they, too, have a story to share.

There is nothing routine or blasé about a home group based around the supernatural ministry of God's mighty Spirit. And once you've tasted the excitement, anticipation, and joy of such a weekly gathering, your vision for small group ministry will change forever!

Epilogue
How Sweet It Is!

WELL-ROUNDED CHRISTIANS WILL worship together, pray together, serve together, give together, learn together, and reach out together.

We can't imagine doing life without our loving church family. We laugh, cry, play, work, pray, worship, celebrate, grieve, assist, learn, and serve together. It makes the journey exciting and fulfilling. We do this by serving at our local church and in our home groups. How sweet it is!

In our introduction, we told of moving to Bend, Oregon in 1998 and beginning a home group with five people from our church. We chronicled their deliverances, healings, growth, and transformation into strong, respected leaders in our church.

Our local MTC has graduated a couple hundred students. Almost without exception, they are serving the church, many in leadership roles. Currently in the Northwest, we have six hundred students enrolled in local church MTCs. It stirs us deeply to think where this is leading!

The dozen small groups here at Westside that have Holy Spirit empowered ministry are healthy and thriving. But the thing that excites us most is the second- and third-generation growth we are experiencing—as when Debbie birthed and coached twenty small groups of teens, raising up leaders who will begin still more groups.

Frankly, we had no idea how extensive the outreach had become from one small home group until we felt led to write this book and began to look at the big picture. Several hundred people are directly involved in this Holy Spirit-directed ministry, and it has happened by organic growth—not through some off-the-shelf program. You, Lord Jesus, are building Your church!

We hope you can see the value of Holy Spirit empowered small groups, and the life-giving force they can become in a local church. These groups work in small, medium, and large churches in America, as well as for thirty village pastors in Malawi living in dirt-floor huts. You see, we all have the same basic needs to be loved, accepted, and forgiven by God and by each other.

In Acts 2, we noted how the people met in the temple courts and from house to house. We believe that same pattern can be successfully followed today. Our weekend celebration services relate to their temple court gatherings, and our Holy Spirit empowered small groups correspond to meeting "house to house."

And what can we expect? Why should we anticipate anything less than what the first church experienced: "And the Lord added to the church daily those who were being saved" (Acts 2:47, NIV).

Yes, that's the answer to our original question in the introduction: "How will the new converts be cared for, nurtured, and discipled when our prayer for a powerful, worldwide awakening is answered?" It will be through Holy Spirit empowered small groups!

Appendix A
Teaching on the Baptism of the Holy Spirit

THE FOLLOWING APPENDIX is a lesson excerpted from the Ambassador Series curriculum. This lesson has been used to lead thousands of believers into this transforming supernatural experience.

In any teaching on the Person and work of the Holy Spirit, we are not only to be concerned with an academic understanding of who He is and what He does. We must also apply that knowledge to our daily life. The Holy Spirit is a Person, and His work in each of our lives is individual, relational, and intensely personal.

Through His ministry in our lives and by His empowering, we become the mouth, hands, and heart of Jesus to the people we meet every day.

THE POWER OF THE HOLY SPIRIT

Promised by Jesus
The Holy Spirit was promised by the Lord Jesus Christ, and Jesus is the One who baptizes His followers with the Holy Spirit. Water baptism demonstrates our obedience to follow Christ. The Holy Spirit baptism gives us the power to do the things our Lord asks us to do.

The people were waiting expectantly and were all wondering in their hearts if John might possibly be the Christ. John answered them all,

> I baptize you *with water*. But one more powerful than I will come, the thongs of whose sandals I am not worthy to untie. *He will baptize you with the Holy Spirit and with fire.*
>
> —LUKE 3:15–16, NIV, EMPHASIS ADDED

> I am going to send you what my Father has promised; but stay in the city until you have been *clothed with power from on high.*
>
> —LUKE 24:49, NIV, EMPHASIS ADDED

> On one occasion, while he was eating with them, he gave them this command: "Do not leave Jerusalem, but wait for the gift my Father promised, which you have heard me speak about. For John baptized with water, but in a few days *you will be baptized with the Holy Spirit.*
>
> —ACTS 1:4–5, NIV, EMPHASIS ADDED

> *But you will receive power* when the Holy Spirit comes on you; and you will be my witnesses in Jerusalem, and in all Judea and Samaria, and to the ends of the earth.
>
> —ACTS 1:8, NIV, EMPHASIS ADDED

Comes upon obedient believers

He will empower us to be effective witnesses. As our Counselor, He gives us guidance. As the Spirit of truth, He brings God's truth. He will never leave us alone; He will always be with believers.

> If you love me, you will obey what I command. And I will ask the Father, and he will give you another Counselor to be with you forever—the Spirit of truth. The world cannot accept him, because it neither sees him nor knows him. But you know him, for he lives with

you and will be in you. I will not leave you as orphans;
I will come to you.

—John 14:15–18, niv

His activity on our behalf

All this I have spoken while still with you. But the Counselor, the Holy Spirit, whom the Father will send in my
name, *will teach you all things and will remind you of
everything I have said to you.*

—John 14:25–26, niv, emphasis added

But I tell you the truth: It is for your good that I am going
away. Unless I go away, the Counselor will not come to
you; but if I go, I will send him to you...I have much
more to say to you, more than you can now bear. But
when he, the Spirit of truth, comes, he will guide you
into all truth.

—John 16:7; 12–13, niv

Now I am going to him who sent me, yet none of you
asks me, 'Where are you going?' Because I have said
these things, you are filled with grief. But I tell you the
truth: It is for your good that I am going away. Unless I
go away, *the Counselor* will not come to you; but if I go,
I will send him to you. When he comes, *he will convict
the world of guilt in regard to sin* and righteousness and
judgment: in regard to sin, because men do not believe
in me; in regard to righteousness, because I am going
to the Father, where you can see me no longer; and in
regard to judgment, because *the prince of this world
now stands condemned.* I have much more to say to you,
more than you can now bear. But when he, the Spirit of
truth, comes, *he will guide you into all truth.* He will not
speak on his own; *he will speak only what he hears,* and
*he will tell you what is yet to come. He will bring glory to
me* by taking from what is mine and making it known
to you. All that belongs to the Father is mine. That is

why I said *the Spirit will take from what is mine and make it known to you.*
—John 16:5–15, NIV, EMPHASIS ADDED

In summary, then, the Spirit of God…

- teaches us all things, helping us to understand what God desires for our lives;

- brings all things to our remembrance, helping us to remember specific scriptures;

- convicts the world of sin, causing sinners to realize they have disobeyed God;

- convinces the world that a new life is possible, offering a fresh start and new life;

- convinces the world that Satan is defeated and condemned, assuring us that the enemy of our souls has been judged and found guilty;

- guides us into all truth, leading us into the very best God has for us;

- speaks to us about things to come, reminding us of what God wants done;

- will always glorify Christ, focusing on the person of Christ, not upon Himself;

- gives us power, enabling us to accomplish the kind of ministry Jesus says we can do.

THE BAPTISM OF THE HOLY SPIRIT

The purpose of Holy Spirit baptism is to be "clothed" with power from heaven to be an effective witness for Jesus Christ.

We received the Holy Spirit *in* us when we first believed, repented, and received Jesus Christ as Lord of our life. At that time, we were "born again" by the Holy Spirit. The baptism in the Holy Spirit is in addition to and separate from that initial new birth experience. It occurs when the Holy Spirit comes *upon* a believer who simply asks Jesus Christ for this matchless gift of love and power.

> I am going to send you what my Father has promised; but stay in the city until you have been clothed with power from on high.
>
> —LUKE 24:49, NIV

> But you will receive power when the Holy Spirit comes on you; and you will be my witnesses in Jerusalem, and in all Judea and Samaria, and to the ends of the earth.
>
> —ACTS 1:8, NIV

Jesus Christ gives the gift of the Holy Spirit

1. The Holy Spirit baptism was promised through Jesus Christ, and this was His message:

> After me will come one more powerful than I, the thongs of whose sandals I am not worthy to stoop down and untie. I baptize you with water, but he [Jesus] will baptize you with the Holy Spirit.
>
> —MARK 1:7–8, NIV

2. The Holy Spirit is WITH us, drawing us to Jesus Christ.

> And I will ask the Father, and he will give you *another Counselor* to be with you forever—the Spirit of truth. The world cannot accept him, because it neither sees him nor knows him. But you know him, for *he lives with you* and will be in you.
>
> —JOHN 14:16–17, NIV, EMPHASIS ADDED

3. The Holy Spirit dwells WITHIN us, upon receiving Jesus Christ.

But you know him, for he lives with you and will be *in* you.
—John 14:17, NIV, EMPHASIS ADDED

4. The Holy Spirit comes UPON us, when we ask Jesus Christ for the gift.

When they arrived, they prayed for them that they might receive the Holy Spirit, because the Holy Spirit had not yet come *upon* any of them; they had simply been baptized into the name of the Lord Jesus. Then Peter and John placed their hands on them, and they received the Holy Spirit.
—Acts 8:15–17, NIV, EMPHASIS ADDED

While Peter was still speaking these words, the Holy Spirit *came on* all who heard the message. The circumcised believers who had come with Peter were astonished that the gift of the Holy Spirit had been poured out even *on* the Gentiles. For they heard them speaking in tongues and praising God. Then Peter said, "Can anyone keep these people from being baptized with water? They have received the Holy Spirit just as we have."
—Acts 10:44–47, NIV, EMPHASIS ADDED

On hearing this, they were baptized into the name of the Lord Jesus. When Paul placed his hands on them, the Holy Spirit came *on* them, and they spoke in tongues and prophesied.
—Acts 19:5–6, NIV, EMPHASIS ADDED

What happens when we ask

1. Jesus Christ always gives the Holy Spirit to those who ask.

For *everyone who asks receives; he who seeks finds; and to him who knocks, the door will be opened.* Which of you fathers, if your son asks for a fish, will give him a snake instead? Or if he asks for an egg, will give him a scorpion? If you then, though you are evil, know how to give good gifts to your children, *how much more will your Father in heaven give the Holy Spirit to those who ask him!*
—LUKE 11:10–13, NIV, EMPHASIS ADDED

2. We receive the gift of the Holy Spirit in the same moment that we ask.

For everyone who asks receives; he who seeks finds.
—LUKE 11:10, NIV, EMPHASIS ADDED

3. We receive a variety of gifts wrapped up in the gift of the Holy Spirit.

There are *different kinds of gifts,* but the same Spirit. There are different kinds of service, but the same Lord. There are different kinds of working, but the same God works all of them in all men. Now to each one the manifestation of the Spirit is given for the common good. To one there is given through the Spirit the message of wisdom, to another the message of knowledge by means of the same Spirit, to another faith by the same Spirit, to another gifts of healing by that one Spirit, to another miraculous powers, to another prophecy, to another distinguishing between spirits, to another *speaking in different kinds of tongues,* and to still another the interpretation of tongues. All these are the work of one and the same Spirit, and he gives them to each one, just as he determines.
—1 CORINTHIANS 12:4–11, NIV, EMPHASIS ADDED

4. One of the gifts, the ability to speak in tongues, is immediately available to any believer who earnestly desires it.

After asking Jesus for the gift of the Holy Spirit, we immediately *respond in faith* by speaking new words of thanksgiving to Him in a language we have not learned. As a *personal confirmation* that we have been baptized in the Holy Spirit, we are then enabled to pray and praise the heavenly Father in a heavenly language.

Biblical reasons for speaking in tongues

1. We all are encouraged to speak in tongues and prophesy.

I would like every one of you to speak in tongues, but I would rather have you prophesy. He who prophesies is greater than one who speaks in tongues, unless he interprets, so that the church may be edified.

—1 CORINTHIANS 14:5, NIV

2. It edifies or "builds up" our inner spirit.

He who speaks in a tongue edifies himself, but he who prophesies edifies the church.

—1 CORINTHIANS 14:4

But you, dear friends, build yourselves up in your most holy faith and pray in the Holy Spirit.

—JUDE 20

3. It allows the Holy Spirit to pray through us according to the will of God.

The Spirit himself intercedes for us with groans that words cannot express…the Spirit intercedes for the saints in accordance with God's will.

—ROMANS 8:26–27, NIV

4. It allows us to enter the realm of the supernatural.

> For if I pray in a tongue, my spirit prays, but my mind is unfruitful. So what shall I do? I will pray with my spirit, but I will also pray with my mind; I will sing with my spirit, but I will also sing with my mind.
>
> —1 CORINTHIANS 14:14–15, NIV

5. It allows us to hear words of instruction from the Lord.

> What then shall we say, brothers? When you come together, everyone has a hymn, or a word of instruction, a revelation, a tongue or an interpretation. All of these must be done for the strengthening of the church.
>
> —1 CORINTHIANS 14:26, NIV

Misunderstandings

This experience has brought much confusion to the body of Christ—primarily because of a lack of proper, consistent teaching. It has now been experienced by believers worldwide in all Christian denominations, yet there are still those who deny its authenticity. Here are three of the primary reasons:

1. It is not necessarily a sign of spirituality; it is a gift for the believer, no matter how young they are in the Lord. A brand new believer can have this experience. Without a proper biblical foundation, some immature believers have inferred to other Christians that they were "more spiritual" because they "spoke in tongues." Wrong, wrong, wrong! There are many very spiritual Christians who have not had this experience. However, if they desire more of the Holy Spirit in their lives, this gift is for them also.

2. Many people equate this experience to "speaking in tongues." As wonderful as this experience is (speaking in *glossolalia*—languages one has not learned), it is only a small part of the total experience. As we will see, the experience is about supernatural power, prayer, edification, and many other dimensions of the Holy Spirit. It is

75

often the introduction for the believer to the supernatural of God and provides insight into the supernatural of Satan as well.

3. People confuse this experience, which is for all believers, with the gifts of "speaking in different kinds of tongues" and "interpretation of tongues," which are discussed by Paul in 1 Corinthians 12:7–11. Speaking in tongues, which all believers can experience, is more of a devotional prayer dimension which Paul refers to in chapter 14 of 1 Corinthians. He even thanks God that he "speaks in tongues" more than all of them. The gifts discussed in the 1 Corinthians 12 passage are for messages from God to the church.

How to lead a believer into the baptism in the Holy Spirit

1. Determine if the person is born again.

2. Determine their motive. If it is simply to speak in tongues, make sure they have a greater understanding before you proceed.

3. Explain that this gift is a free gift just like salvation. You receive the gift the moment you ask in faith believing, just like salvation.

4. Hindrances: Incomplete or wrong teaching, unforgiveness, or occult practices. Give them a Scriptural understanding and lead them in prayer about these matters before proceeding.

5. Explain exactly what you are going to do.

6. The person then prays and asks the Lord Jesus Christ for the gift of the Holy Spirit and the ability to speak in languages they have not learned.

7. Reassure them that they will receive the moment they ask.

8. Instruct them to take a deep breath and allow the Holy Spirit to give them the words. The best description is that it may sound like a baby learning to talk in the beginning; nonsensical syllables. Jesus asks us to become like little trusting children—speaking words of praise to the Heavenly Father. We simply speak the words the Holy Spirit prompts. What it sounds like is up to Him.

9. Put your hand lightly on the person's shoulder and pray softly in your own prayer language. Don't be in a hurry. Give the person a few moments. Gently encourage them to not be afraid nor care what it sounds like. They will begin speaking, and you simply keep encouraging them and validating their experience.

10. Finally, encourage them to pray in their new language as often as possible, but to not get "religious" about it. Pray riding in the car, taking walks, or any other activity which lends itself to prayer.

11. Summary of speaking in tongues from 1 Corinthians 14:

- It is a real language.

- It is speaking to God.

- It is speaking spiritual secrets.

- It is being personally built up.

- It is my spirit praying through the Holy Spirit.

- It is giving thanks well.

Appendix B
Thirteen-Week Small Group Study

For pastors

It is imperative that qualified leaders be used to begin the groups. By "qualified," we mean Christians who have been baptized in the Holy Spirit, have authentic experiences in the supernatural gifts of the Holy Spirit, and a passion to lead a group of this nature. There are literally hundreds of thousands of people sitting in our churches with this kind of experience that need to be mobilized. If you do not have any experienced people in the congregation available, then perhaps you should mentor some leaders that would qualify. We strongly recommend using practical discipleship approaches that major in hands-on, real-life practicum sessions that provide biblical experiences that can be reproduced in others.[1]

If your small groups (minichurches or cell groups) are stagnant with little growth and without life-giving testimonies, perhaps this approach is what is needed to breathe life into them—the Zoë life of the Holy Spirit.

When suitable leaders have been identified, then the following thirteen lessons can be used to launch a Holy Spirit empowered small group.

For small groups leaders

Before the first meeting, pray, and then contact a few Christians you think might be interested in this type of a small group. The others might also know of a person or two to invite. If you begin with five or six core people in addition to yourselves, then there is room for guests each week. It would be good to have copies of this book available for interested people, or tell them where they can purchase a copy. As leaders, you might want to read Chapter Three, "Small Group Anatomy," before the meeting so you will know where we are ultimately headed.

Establish a weekly time and place. You are now ready to begin a spiritual journey that can be a life-changing experience for you and the people who attend the gathering. You will have success if you follow what we have already proven to be the most effective format and content for a thirteen-week exposure to the supernatural moving of the Holy Spirit in a small group setting.

WEEK ONE

Once again, refer to Chapter Three, "Small Group Anatomy." Always pray the day prior to the small group meeting for inspiration from the Holy Spirit regarding what He may want to do in addition to (or instead of) what you have planned. With this in mind, we are always ready to defer to whatever the Holy Spirit wants to do. For the sake of this chapter, let's assume we have peace about what we have planned for the meeting.

Refreshments (15 minutes)

Begin with a fifteen-minute, get-acquainted time over refreshments. Start with veggies, chips, cookies, sodas, tea, and coffee. This will allow everyone to arrive, get acquainted, fellowship, and get settled. Have name tags for everyone to fill out and a visitor's book to record the names and phone numbers of everyone attending.

Worship (10 minutes)

Find someone who plays guitar or keyboards at your church who would be willing to become a part of your small group. All churches have musicians and worship leaders that may be just learning or don't have opportunities to be on the regular worship team. (This is a wonderful way for them to gain experience while they bless the small group. We have personally raised up several people in this way.) Have them lead not more than three simple choruses each week, starting at fifteen minutes past the hour. If none is available, have a "music person" lead the choruses a cappella. Always keep within the ten-minute time frame.

Introductions (20 minutes)

Begin by welcoming everyone, explaining that this will be a get-acquainted evening. Set the stage by giving a short background about yourselves. It could be something like this:

> We are John and Sonja Decker. We have lived in Bend about eight years and have attended Westside Church for the same amount of time. Small groups have always been a very positive experience for us. We've been in them for over thirty years. In fact, we both found out we had teaching gifts in the small group setting, and that's what we do now—leadership training for churches. We are sure looking forward to getting to know all of you. We would like each one of you to introduce yourselves so we can get to know you.

It would be appropriate at this time to explain the absolute necessity that the group hold confidences and make this a safe place for all who attend. We always try to structure our meetings so everyone has opportunity to share something each week. We have purposed to do this so everyone feels a part of what is going on.

We would start the first week by simply asking everyone to introduce themselves by giving his or her name, what part of town they live in, what church they attend (you can't assume they are from your church), and how they found out about the group. We suggest group leaders always ask non-invasive questions of the guests, so they can easily feel part of the group.

Sharing (30 minutes)

After everyone has been introduced and has spoken a little about themselves, ask the group to open to the Introduction of this book. Read the first two pages, so you can discuss it as a group. After reading the Introduction, start the discussion by posing some questions about what was read. Here are sample questions you might use:

> 1. Do you believe a worldwide revival and awakening will happen in your lifetime?
>
> 2. What do you think about what Jesus said in Matthew 9:36–38?
>
> But when He saw the multitudes, He was moved with compassion for them, because they were weary and scattered, like sheep having no shepherd. Then He said to His disciples, "The harvest truly is plentiful, but the laborers are few. Therefore pray the Lord of the harvest to send out laborers into His harvest."
>
> 3. Do you feel we could be those laborers?
>
> 4. Do you think it would be exciting to have people come to our group and be introduced to the Lord Jesus Christ?

Allow everyone ample time to contribute to the discussion. Watch for the "quiet" ones, asking if they have anything to add to what is being said. Following this thirty-minute segment, prepare to transition into the "ministry time."

Ministry Time (45 minutes)

Prior to asking for any prayer concerns from the group, explain how the prayer ministry time will work. First, explain that the goal of this part of the meeting is to allow the Holy Spirit freedom to meet people's physical, emotional, and spiritual needs. Everyone should remain sensitive and expectant toward the Lord to meet those needs. Second, everyone is encouraged to join with the group leaders by helping to pray and minister over the others requesting prayer. The leaders should encourage such things as the "laying on of hands," praying loudly enough so everyone can hear, and even exercising individual spiritual languages when appropriate.

Invite everyone to participate at his or her own comfort level. Start this portion of the meeting by asking the group for any prayer requests. "Is there anyone who would like prayer for anything?" Have those who are close place their hands on the shoulders of whoever responds, and pray for God to meet the need. Continue ministering this way to each person requesting prayer until there are no more requests.

Explain that the group will be learning more about how to pray in the coming weeks. The ministry time should take the remainder of the time, about forty-five minutes.

Assignment for next week

Ask everyone to read the remaining pages of the introduction to this book during the week. Close the meeting with a short prayer of thanks for what has transpired. Always end on time.

WEEK TWO

Refreshments (15 minutes)

Put out the veggies, chips, cookies, rolls, juice, coffee, sodas, etc. If anyone offers to bring refreshments, suggest the group take turns bringing something each week. The host home should always provide the drinks. Be sure everyone fills out a name tag each week. This is especially important if any first-timers show up. Greet everyone warmly, and offer them refreshments. Inform them that formal introductions will start in a few minutes when everyone is seated.

Worship (10 minutes)

Have the music person lead not more than three simple choruses, keeping within the ten-minute time frame.

Introductions (20 minutes)

Start with a short prayer, asking for the Lord's presence and guidance for the evening. Welcome everyone, and tell the group to expect God to meet with them in a tangible way. Start the introductions by giving a brief background about yourselves, similar to the first week. It could be something like this:

> We are John and Sonja Decker. We attend Westside Church. Small groups have always been a very positive experience for us over the last thirty years. We are sure looking forward to getting to know everyone better. We would like each one of you to introduce yourselves again so we can get to know you.

As in the previous week's outline, we always try to structure our meetings so everyone has opportunity to share something each week. For this second week, ask people to introduce themselves by giving his or her name, where they live, and *when they first knew for sure they were going to heaven*. The leaders should inform the guests that this part of the meeting is where we get to know everyone better. We ask a get-acquainted question that everyone, including the guests, can answer.

Sharing (30 minutes)

After everyone has been introduced and has shared about themselves by responding to the question, ask the group to open to the Introduction of this book. Briefly provide a basic overview of the contents to the guests. Begin the discussion by posing the following sample questions:

84

1. Do you or someone you know have a similar family situation like the Roper family? If so, please share about it.

2. Do you think John 14:12 is applicable for us today? What are some of the "works" Jesus was referring to?

3. What are some of the things our small group could do to make it a "place of refuge and safety?"

4. Regarding the story of the single mom related in the Introduction, do you know of a single mom in a similar situation? If so, do you think she would benefit by coming to this group? Would you like to invite her?

5. Regarding the young Marine, is there anyone in the group who desires to know more about the same experience with the Holy Spirit?

Allow everyone ample time to respond and contribute to the discussion. Continue to encourage the "quiet" ones, asking if they have anything to add to what is being said. Try to keep this part of the meeting to thirty minutes, then prepare to transition into the "ministry time."

Ministry Time (45 minutes)

Again, the small group leader explains how the ministry time will work. The goal of this part of the meeting is to allow the Holy Spirit freedom to meet people's physical, emotional, and spiritual needs. Everyone should remain sensitive and expectant towards the Lord to meet those needs. Also, everyone should be encouraged to join in by helping to pray and minister over the people requesting prayer. The leaders should encourage the "laying on of hands," praying loudly enough so everyone can hear, and even exercising individual spiritual languages when appropriate. Invite everyone to participate at his or her own comfort level. Begin by asking the group for any specific prayer requests such as:

- Is there anyone who would like prayer for healing?

- Is there anyone with an urgent personal need we can pray for?

- Is there anyone needing an answer and/or confirmation from the Lord?

When a supernatural word of knowledge or wisdom is revealed to anyone gathered, the person having the word should get the attention of the leader by saying; "I believe I have a word for someone (name the person if known). May I share it?" The leader then has the prerogative to allow or disallow the word to be spoken, depending on how well the leader knows the person. This little ground rule should be announced as the group moves into the ministry time.

Have everyone place their hands on the shoulders of whoever is requesting ministry and pray for God to meet the need. Continue ministering this way until there are no more requests. Explain that the group will experience different ways to pray in the coming weeks. The ministry time should take the remainder of the meeting, about forty-five minutes.

Assignment for next week

- Read chapter one, "Jesus Loves Small Groups."

- Be ready to discuss the principles found in this chapter. End on time.

WEEK THREE

Refreshments (15 minutes)

Put out the veggies, chips, cookies, rolls, juice, coffee, sodas, etc. Thank those that bring refreshments each week. The host home should always provide the drinks. Be sure everyone fills out a name tag each time you gather. This is especially important if any first-timers show up. Greet everyone with a hug and offer them refreshments. Inform them that formal introductions will start in a few minutes after everyone is seated.

Worship (10 minutes)

As with previous weeks, have the music person lead not more than three simple choruses, keeping within the ten-minute time frame.

Introductions (20 minutes)

Start with a short prayer, asking for the Lord's presence. Welcome everyone, and tell the group to expect God to meet with them in a tangible way. The leaders start the introductions by asking everyone to introduce themselves by stating their names, where they live, and *when they thought they heard the voice of the Lord*. The leaders should inform the guests that this part of the meeting is where we get to know everyone better. We ask a get-acquainted question that everyone, including the guests, can answer.

Sharing (30 minutes)

Ask the group to open to Chapter One, "Jesus Loves Small Groups." Briefly provide a basic overview of the chapter to the guests. Begin the discussion by posing the sample questions such as these:

1. What part of Matthew 18:19–20 can be fulfilled by attending a small group?

2. What can be accomplished in a small group that is difficult to do in a normal Sunday service?

3. Can you list three or more things that the Holy Spirit will minister through the members of a small group?

4. Look at the section titled, "Without Guile." Is dealing with spiritual bondages something we should learn how

to do? Where would be the best place to learn about it? Allow everyone ample time to respond and contribute to the discussion. Continue to encourage the "quiet" ones to participate. Keep this part of the meeting to thirty minutes, then prepare to transition into the "ministry time."

Ministry Time (45 minutes)

Again, everyone should remain sensitive and expectant toward the Lord to meet the needs of those present. Also, everyone needs to join in the ministry by praying and ministering to those needing prayer. The leaders should encourage the "laying on of hands," praying loudly enough so everyone can hear, and even exercising individual spiritual languages when appropriate. Invite everyone to participate at his or her own comfort level. The leaders should model receiving and acting on words of knowledge and wisdom and encouraging group members to do the same. These words should be released in the same manner as outlined in Week Two.

Begin by asking the group for any personal prayer requests such as:

- Is there anyone who would like prayer for healing?

- Is there anyone with an urgent personal need we can pray for?

- Who needs direction or a confirming word from the Lord?

- Is there a word from the Lord anyone would like to share?

Prayer requests for someone not present (intercession) should be held until all personal needs of those present have received prayer.

Assignment for next week

- Read chapter two, "Let's Do It Jesus' Way."

- Be ready to discuss the principles found in this chapter. End on time.

WEEK FOUR

Refreshments (15 minutes)

As in previous weeks, have the refreshments, coffee, and name tags ready before the people arrive.

Worship (10 minutes)

Have the music person lead not more than three simple choruses, keeping within the ten-minute time frame.

Introductions (20 minutes)

Start with a short prayer, asking for the Lord's presence. Welcome everyone, encouraging those gathered to expect God to meet with them in a tangible way. The leaders start the introductions, asking everyone to introduce themselves by stating their names, where they live, *when they were baptized in the Holy Spirit and what this experience did for them.* The leaders should inform the guests that this part of the meeting is where we get to know everyone better. We ask a get-acquainted question that everyone, including the guests, can answer.

Sharing (30 minutes)

Ask everyone to open to chapter two, "Let's Do It Jesus' Way." Briefly provide a basic overview of the chapter to the guests. Begin the discussion by posing questions similar to these:

1. Can you give some examples of Christians you have seen exhibiting "weird" behavior and attributing it to being spiritual?

2. The lady mentioned in "A Curious Believer" was healed by responding to a word of knowledge, as described in 1 Corinthians 12:8. Has anyone witnessed this type of thing happening recently? Explain.

3. Would anyone here like to have God use them in speaking words of prophecy, words of knowledge, words of wisdom, or discerning of spirits (see 1 Corinthians 12:8–10)? Where would be the most likely place to learn how to do these things? How should it be done?

4. Look at the section entitled, "Under Spiritual Authority." How important is it to have small group leadership exercise firm spiritual guidance and/or correction during the ministry times?

Ministry Time (45 minutes)

Again, everyone should remain sensitive and expectant toward the Lord to meet the needs of those present. Begin by asking the guests if they have any needs the group can pray for. Also, everyone needs to join in the ministry by praying and ministering to the people needing prayer. The leaders should encourage the "laying on of hands," praying loudly enough so everyone can hear, and even exercising individual spiritual languages when appropriate. Invite everyone to participate at his or her own comfort level. The leaders should model receiving and acting on words of knowledge and wisdom, encouraging the others to do the same. These words should be released in the same manner as outlined in Week Two.

Continue by asking the group for any testimonies or answers to prayer from last week's ministry time. After sharing answers to prayer, ask the group for personal prayer requests, such as:

- Is there a word of revelation from the Holy Spirit? Would anyone like to share what the Lord may want to say to the group?

- Is there anyone who would like prayer for healing?

- Is there anyone with an urgent personal need we can pray for?

- Is there anyone seeking a confirming word from the Lord?

- Are there any other prayer needs for someone you know that needs God to intervene in their life?

Assignment for next week

- Read chapter three, "Small Group Anatomy."

- Be ready to discuss the principles found in this chapter.

- Ask everyone to consider bringing a guest next week. End on time.

WEEK FIVE

Refreshments (15 minutes)
Have the refreshments, coffee, and name tags ready before the people arrive.

Worship (10 minutes)
Have the music person lead not more than three simple choruses, keeping within the ten-minute time frame.

Introductions (20 minutes)
Start with a short prayer, asking for the Lord's presence. Welcome everyone, and tell the group to expect God to meet with them in a tangible way. The leaders start the introductions by asking everyone to introduce themselves by stating their names and where they live. Read 1 Corinthians 14:26 and ask, "What did you bring to give away to the group tonight?" The leaders

should inform the guests that this part of the meeting is where we get to know everyone better. We ask a get-acquainted question that everyone, including the guests, can answer.

Sharing (30 minutes)

Ask everyone to open to chapter three, "Small Group Anatomy." Briefly provide a basic overview of the chapter to the guests. Begin the sharing by posing the following sample questions:

> 1. What type of small group do you prefer—a structured Bible study, an intercessory prayer meeting, or a Holy Spirit empowered ministry group like we are experiencing here. Discuss why.

> 2. Would it be too radical to invite a pre-Christian (anyone who does not personally know Christ) to this small group? What do you think would happen if they showed up here next week?

> 3. What is the main barrier in Christian minds that prevents us from inviting pre-Christians to a small group?

> 4. Why do you think Holy Spirit empowered small groups tend to multiply faster than other types of small groups? Explain.

> 5. Regarding the story in the section entitled, "Bridge to Hope," what part of the MTC training appeals to you, if any?

Ministry Time (45 minutes)

Begin by asking the group for any testimonies or answers to prayer from last week's ministry time. After sharing answers to prayer, ask the group for personal prayer requests such as healing, bondages, addictions, direction for their life, spiritual confusion, or spiritual warfare issues. With the leaders directing the ministry, everyone participates. The leaders should not be the ones initiating all of the actual "hands-on" part of the prayer ministry. The leaders see that the others do the praying, including the newcomers who have not experienced this kind of prayer ministry. The leaders should encourage the "laying on of hands," praying loudly enough so everyone can hear, and even exercising praying in tongues (spiritual languages). The leaders should model praying quietly in tongues and receiving and acting on words of knowledge and wisdom and encourage the others to do the same.

Mention that the group will be studying the gifts of the Spirit next week. Any "words" or revelation assumed to be from the Holy Spirit are subject to critique or judging according to 1 Corinthians 14:29–32. When the words are deemed appropriate, they are then shared with the people for whom they are intended. Finally, the people receiving the words should tell the group whether the words confirm or "fit" their situation.

Assignment for next week

- Read chapter four, "Releasing Gifts of the Holy Spirit."

- Be ready to discuss the principles found in this chapter.

- Ask everyone to consider bringing a guest next week. End on time.

WEEK SIX

Refreshments (15 minutes)
Have the refreshments, coffee, and name tags ready before the people arrive.

Worship (10 minutes)
Have the music person lead not more than three simple choruses, keeping within the ten-minute time frame.

Introductions (20 minutes)

Start with a short prayer, asking for the Lord's presence. Welcome everyone, and tell the group to expect God to meet with them in a tangible way. The leaders start the introductions by asking everyone to introduce themselves by stating their names and where they live. According to 1 Corinthians 14:26, ask them, "Are you aware of any gifts of the Holy Spirit that are active in your life?" The leaders should inform the guests that this part of the meeting is where we get to know everyone better. We ask a get-acquainted question that everyone, including the guests, can answer.

Sharing (30 minutes)

Ask everyone to open to chapter four, "Releasing Gifts of the Holy Spirit." Briefly provide a basic overview of the chapter to the guests. Begin the sharing by posing questions such as these:

1. How many in this small group have responded to Jesus' command to be baptized in the Holy Spirit, according to Acts 1:4–8? How do you know for sure that the gift of the Holy Spirit is upon your life?

2. Are there any here tonight that would like to share how the Lord has used them to minister gifts of the Holy Spirit to others?

3. Do any of you know any "charismatic Christians"?

4. Would you agree with the assertion that our youth have a desperate hunger for the reality of the supernatural power of God? What do we need to do to channel and disciple them into the supernatural power of God?

Ministry Time (45 minutes)

Begin by asking the group for any testimonies or answers to prayer from last week's ministry time. After sharing answers to prayer, ask the group for personal prayer requests such as healing, bondages, addictions, direction for their life, spiritual confusion, or spiritual warfare issues. With the leaders directing the ministry, everyone participates. The leaders should not be the ones initiating all of the actual "hands-on" part of the prayer ministry. Instead, the leaders should see to it that others do the praying, including newcomers who have not experienced this kind of prayer ministry. The leaders should encourage the "laying on of hands," praying loudly enough so everyone can hear, and even exercising praying in tongues (spiritual languages). The leaders should model praying quietly in tongues and receiving and acting on "words" of knowledge and wisdom, and encourage the others to do the same.

Any words or revelation assumed to be from the Holy Spirit are subject to critique or judging according to 1 Corinthians 14:29–32. When the words are deemed appropriate, they are then shared with the people for whom they are intended. Finally, the people receiving the words should tell the group whether the words confirm or "fit" their situation.

Assignment for next week

- Read chapter five, "What Do They Have in Common?"

- Be ready to discuss the principles found in this chapter.

- Ask everyone to consider bringing a guest next week. End on time.

WEEK SEVEN

Refreshments (15 minutes)
Have the refreshments, coffee, and name tags ready before the people arrive.

Worship (10 minutes)

Have the music person lead not more than three simple choruses, keeping within the ten-minute time frame.

Introductions (20 minutes)

Start with a short prayer, asking for the Lord's presence. Welcome everyone, and tell the group to expect God to meet with them in a tangible way. The leaders start the introductions by asking everyone to introduce themselves by stating their names and where they live. Then ask the group, "What would you like to have God do so you could experience Him up close and personal?" The leaders should inform the guests that this part of the meeting is where we get to know everyone better. We ask a get-acquainted question that everyone, including the guests, can answer.

Sharing (30 minutes)

Ask everyone to open to chapter five, "What Do They Have in Common?" Briefly provide a basic overview of the chapter to the guests. Begin the sharing by posing the following sample questions:

1. As we look at everyone gathered here tonight, what is the one thing that motivates us to keep coming back each week? Everybody can respond to this question in his or her own words.

2. Can each of you think of at least one person that would enjoy what we are experiencing in this group? Do you think they would come if you invited them? How about next week?

3. Do you know of any seventeen-year-olds who have a testimony similar to the story about Whitney in "Erasing Generational Barriers"?

4. Would this group like to do what was done in the stories of the impoverished man released from prison?

Ministry Time (45 minutes)

Begin by asking the group for any testimonies or answers to prayer from last week's ministry time. After sharing answers to prayer, ask the group (including guests) for personal prayer requests such as healing, bondages, addictions, direction for their life, spiritual confusion, or spiritual warfare issues. With the leaders directing the ministry, everyone participates. The leaders should not be the ones initiating all of the actual "hands-on" part of the prayer ministry. The leaders see that the others do the praying, including newcomers who have not experienced this kind of prayer ministry. The leaders should encourage the "laying on of hands," praying loudly enough so everyone can hear, and even exercising praying in tongues (spiritual languages). The leaders should model praying quietly in tongues and receiving and acting on words of knowledge and wisdom, and encourage the others to do the same. Any words or revelation assumed to be from the Holy Spirit are subject to critique or judging according to 1 Corinthians 14:29–32. When the words are deemed appropriate, they are then shared with the people for whom they are intended. Finally, the people receiving the words should tell the group whether the words confirm or "fit" their situation.

Assignment for next week

- Read the first part of chapter six, "Healed and Set Free" up to the section entitled, "Judy K.'s Story."

- Be ready to discuss the principles found in this part of chapter six.

- Ask everyone to consider bringing a guest next week. As always, make it a priority to end on time.

Week Eight

Refreshments (15 minutes)

Have the refreshments, coffee, and name tags ready before the people arrive.

Worship (10 minutes)

Have the music person lead not more than three simple choruses, keeping within the ten-minute time frame.

Introductions (20 minutes)

Start with a short prayer, asking for the Lord's presence. Welcome everyone, and tell the group to expect God to meet with them in a tangible way. The leaders start the introductions by asking everyone to introduce themselves by stating their names, where they live, and ask them to tell about *when they have been healed or set free by the Lord*. The leaders should inform the guests that this part of the meeting is where we get to know everyone better. We ask a get-acquainted question that everyone, including the guests, can answer.

Sharing (30 minutes)

Ask everyone to open to chapter six, "Healed and Set Free," and go to the section entitled, "Judy K's Story." Briefly provide a basic overview of this part of the chapter to the guests. Begin the sharing by posing the following sample questions:

1. Assuming that you believe in divine healing from God, what were the main things that finally convinced you it was for today? (Each person can respond to this question.)

2. If God personally has healed you, please explain the circumstances surrounding the event?

3. According to Matthew 10:1, which diseases and sicknesses will the Lord *not* heal? How about fibromyalgia?

Ministry Time (45 minutes)

Begin by asking the group—newcomers included—for any testimonies or answers to prayer from last week's ministry time. After sharing answers to prayer, ask the group for personal prayer requests such as healing, bondages, addictions, direction for their life, spiritual confusion, or spiritual warfare issues. With the leaders directing the ministry, everyone participates. The leaders should not be the ones initiating all of the actual "hands-on" part of the prayer ministry. The leaders see that the others do the praying, including newcomers who have not experienced this kind of prayer ministry. The leaders should encourage the "laying on of hands," praying loudly enough so everyone can hear, and even exercising praying in tongues (spiritual languages). The leaders should model praying quietly in tongues and receiving and acting on words of knowledge and wisdom, and encourage the others to do the same. Any "words" or revelation assumed to be from the Holy Spirit are subject to critique or judging according to 1 Corinthians 14:29–32. When the words are deemed appropriate, they are then shared with the people for whom they are intended. Finally, the people receiving the words should tell the group whether the words confirm or "fit" their situation.

Assignment for next week

- Read the remaining part of chapter six, "Healed and Set Free," from "Judy K.'s Story" to the end of the chapter.

- Be ready to discuss the principles found in this portion of chapter six.

- Ask everyone to consider bringing a guest next week. End on time.

WEEK NINE

Refreshments (15 minutes)

Have the refreshments, coffee, and name tags ready before the people arrive.

Worship (10 minutes)

Have the music person lead not more than three simple choruses, keeping within the ten-minute time frame.

Introductions (20 minutes)

Start with a short prayer, asking for the Lord's presence. Welcome everyone, and tell the group to expect God to meet with them in a tangible way. The leaders start the introductions by asking everyone to introduce themselves by stating their names, where they live, and ask them to tell about when they prayed or ministered to someone needing to be healed and what happened. The leaders should inform the guests that this part of the meeting is where we get to know everyone better. We ask a get-acquainted question that everyone, including the guests, can answer.

Sharing (30 minutes)

Ask everyone to open to the final section of chapter six, "Healed and Set Free," beginning with "Judy K.'s Story" to the end of the chapter. Briefly provide a basic overview of this section to the guests. Begin the sharing by posing the following sample questions:

> 1. Has anyone here ever prayed or ministered to someone needing healing outside of church or this small group? If so, please tell us what happened. Everyone having a testimony like this can share.

> 2. What do you feel is the main reason why we hesitate to minister healing in the marketplace? Are there other reasons for not doing this?

3. Has anyone here ever ministered healing to a pre-Christian? If so, tell us about it.

4. Where do we go to get enough experience and confidence to minister healing to both believers and pre-Christians?

Ministry Time (45 minutes)

Begin by asking the group for any testimonies or answers to prayer from last week's ministry time. After sharing answers to prayer, ask the group for personal prayer requests such as healing, bondages, addictions, direction for their life, spiritual confusion, or spiritual warfare issues. With the leaders directing the ministry, everyone participates. The leaders should not be the ones initiating all of the actual "hands-on" part of the prayer ministry. The leaders see that the others do the praying, including newcomers who have not experienced this kind of prayer ministry. The leaders should encourage the "laying on of hands," praying loudly enough so everyone can hear, and even exercising praying in tongues (spiritual languages).

The leaders should model praying quietly in tongues and receiving and acting on words of knowledge and wisdom, and encourage the others to do the same. Any words or revelation assumed to be from the Holy Spirit are subject to critique or judging according to 1 Corinthians 14:29–32. When the words are deemed appropriate, they are then shared with the people for whom they are intended. Finally, the people receiving the words should tell the group whether the words confirm or "fit" their situation.

Assignment for next week

- Read the final section of this book entitled, "Epilogue: How Sweet It Is!"

- Be ready to discuss the comments the authors have made.

- Ask everyone to consider bringing a guest next week. End on time.

Week Ten

Refreshments (15 minutes)
Have the refreshments, coffee, and name tags ready before the people arrive.

Worship (10 minutes)
Have the music person lead not more than three simple choruses, keeping within the ten-minute time frame.

Introductions (20 minutes)
Start with a short prayer, asking for the Lord's presence. Welcome everyone, and tell the group to expect God to meet with them in a tangible way. The leaders start the introductions by asking everyone to introduce themselves by stating their names, where they live, and ask them to tell about *what they like best about doing life together in this kind of small group.* The leaders should inform the guests that this part of the meeting is where we get to know everyone better. We ask a get-acquainted question that everyone, including the guests, can answer.

Sharing (30 minutes)
Ask everyone to open to the final section of this book entitled, "Epilogue: How Sweet It Is!" Briefly provide a basic overview of the contents. Begin the sharing by posing the following sample questions:

1. This small group has now met for ten weeks. What has been the most rewarding and meaningful personal experience you have enjoyed? Each person should share.

2. What would you recommend the group do differently? Why?

3. Would you recommend this kind of small group for discipling, caring and nurturing of new converts to Christ?

4. Would anyone here like to be trained to start your own Holy Spirit empowered small group? When would you like to start the group? (Those responding can be considered "apprentice-leaders" for the next three weeks of this small group.)

Ministry Time (45 minutes)

Remain consistent: Do exactly the same kind of ministry that has transpired the last nine weeks. Refer back to week nine if needed.

Assignment for next week

- Read chapter 14 of 1 Corinthians.

- Be prepared to share your thoughts about any of the passages.

- Bring your Bible next week.

- Please consider bringing a guest next week. End on time.

Week Eleven

Refreshments (15 minutes)

Have the refreshments, coffee, and name tags ready before the people arrive.

Worship (10 minutes)

Have the music person lead not more than three simple choruses, keeping within the ten-minute time frame.

Introductions (20 minutes)

Open in prayer, and do the introductions the way they have been done the previous weeks. In addition to stating their names and where they live, ask each person to respond to, *"When was the last time you exercised your spiritual language?"* (Speaking in tongues.) The leaders should inform the guests that this part of the meeting is where we get to know everyone better. We ask a get-acquainted question that everyone, including the guests, can answer.

Sharing (30 minutes)

Ask everyone to open his or her Bible to 1 Corinthians 14. Begin the sharing by asking the following sample questions:

> 1. How are speaking in tongues and prophecy useful in today's Christian gatherings?
>
> 2. What passages, if any, seem difficult to understand and apply to this small group? Discuss thoroughly.
>
> 3. First Corinthians 14:14–15 encourages us to both pray and sing in tongues. Would any of you in this setting like to learn how to do this?
>
> 4. Verses 1–5 indicate that one who prophesies edifies those gathered. Would any of you be interested in learning how to prophesy in this setting? When would be the best time to learn these things?

Ministry Time (45 minutes)

Do exactly the same kind of ministry that has transpired the last ten weeks. Encourage everyone to exercise their spiritual language when they minister over those asking for prayer. Also encourage those with a word of prophecy to release it during the ministry time.

Assignment for next week

- Read John 5:19 and 1 Corinthians 12:8,10.

- Be prepared to share your thoughts regarding Jesus'

relationship with the Father and how He acted on what the Father revealed.

- Also, be prepared to share if you have experienced any of the revelation gifts listed in 1 Corinthians 12:8,10.

- Bring your Bible next week.

- Please consider bringing a guest next week. End on time.

WEEK TWELVE

Refreshments (15 minutes)
Have the refreshments, coffee, and name tags ready before the people arrive.

Worship (10 minutes)
Have the music person lead not more than three simple choruses, keeping within the ten-minute time frame.

Introductions (20 minutes)
Open in prayer, and do the introductions the way they have been done the previous weeks. In addition to stating their names and where they live, ask each person to respond to, "When have you heard from God and how did He speak to you?" The leaders should inform the guests that this part of the meeting is where we get to know everyone better. We ask a get-acquainted question that everyone, including the guests, can answer.

Sharing (30 minutes)
Ask everyone to open his or her Bible to John 5:19 and 1 Corinthians 12:8,10. Begin the sharing by asking the following sample questions:

1. Ask everyone to share their thoughts regarding how

Jesus did only what He saw the Father doing and how this directed His ministry to the sick and needy. Share how and why you think He did this.

2. First Corinthians 12:8,10 refers to the revelation gifts as the word of knowledge, the word of wisdom, and the discerning of spirits. Has anyone here been used in these revelation gifts? How did it take place?

3. How many here would like to release the gifts of words of knowledge, wisdom, and discerning of spirits? If so, let's pray this prayer together:

Lord Jesus, I would like to minister in the power and revelation of the Holy Spirit. I thank You that Your gifts are freely given to those who ask. I ask You now to activate the revelation gifts in my life. Thank You for empowering me and giving me the ability to see what the Father wants me to do. I will obey what You reveal for me to do. In Jesus' name I pray. Amen.

Ministry Time (45 minutes)

Do exactly the same kind of ministry that has transpired the last eleven weeks. Encourage everyone to exercise their spiritual language when they minister and exercise the revelation gifts as they pray over those asking for prayer. Words of prophecy should also be released during the worship time and during the ministry time.

Assignment for next week

- Read John 14:12–14.

- Be prepared to share your thoughts regarding how you personally can and should be doing what Jesus did.

- Bring your Bible next week.

- Please consider bringing a guest next week. End on time.

WEEK THIRTEEN

Refreshments (15 minutes)

Have the refreshments, coffee, and name tags ready before the people arrive.

Worship (10 minutes)

Have the music person lead not more than three worship choruses, keeping within the ten-minute time frame. Towards the end of the worship time, encourage singing in the Spirit, prophecy, and the release of the revelation gifts during the worship time.

Introductions (20 minutes)

Open in prayer, and do the introductions the way they have been done the previous weeks. In addition to stating their names and where they live, ask each person to respond to, "Do you feel you are starting to do the things Jesus said you could do?" The leaders should inform the guests that this part of the meeting is where we get to know everyone better. We ask a get-acquainted question that everyone, including the guests, can answer.

Sharing (30 minutes)

Ask everyone to open his or her Bible to John 14:12–14. Begin the sharing by asking the following sample questions:

1. Do you believe Jesus meant it when He said, "You can do what I did"?

2. Share your thoughts regarding how you foresee doing the things Jesus said you could do. Everyone can share.

3. Since Jesus could do only what He saw the Father doing, do you feel you should learn how to do that?

Where do you think this kind of training could best be done?

4. Do you want to start learning how to hear God's instructions? Where do you think this kind of ministry could be learned?

Ministry Time (45 minutes)

Do exactly the same kind of ministry that has transpired the last twelve weeks. Encourage everyone to exercise their spiritual language when they minister and exercise the revelation gifts as they pray over those asking for prayer. Words of prophecy should be released any time deemed appropriate. Encourage everyone to do what has been heard, seen, and done the last twelve weeks.

Assignment

Keep going! If there has been a constant flow of guests, by now your small group has more than tripled in size. It is time to think about birthing one or two more groups. It is recommended that this kind of small group birth another group as soon as the original group feels cramped for space (about four to six months).

By having the new groups start on another night, the new leaders can still attend the original group and not feel they are missing anything. Eventually the excitement in the new group will cause a bonding and healthy anticipation of its own. The fellowship and enthusiasm will equal or exceed what they experienced in the original group.

APPRENTICE LEADERS

During week ten, we encourage potential "apprentice-leaders" to identify themselves and start looking forward to conducting their own Holy Spirit empowered small group. This is the time to encourage them to do that. By now, they have enough experience and knowledge to do it right, thereby setting themselves up for success. If they follow the same thirteen-week process outlined in this book, the Lord will help them with the details of growth and expansion.

Small group leaders who have been mentored in small group settings where healings and miracles are a natural part of the schedule will expect the same when they start their own small group. As the networks of these kinds of groups multiply, it is imperative that teams of knowledgeable, faith-filled disciples spin off into new groups.

Six is an ideal discipleship "core" group to begin an effective small group that will grow and multiply. We started with seven people. In six years we have birthed twelve groups with about six or more experienced "core" believers functioning in the supernatural, using the same format we used. We suggest groups start with six believers, leaving lots of room for guests.

ONGOING HEALING

To have healings continue to occur on a regular basis, we need two things in our groups. First, we need leadership that can hear and obey the Holy Spirit. Second, we need a constant flow of guests needing healing or having other urgent needs. Guests needing healing will come and go. The leadership "core" will remain and set the pace for expansion.

Get ready to see God move in these kinds of small groups! Together, we will witness ordinary Christians moving into the realm of the miraculous as they truly do what Jesus said they could do. People all over the globe are hungering for this kind of training, fellowship, and equipping.

Let's not keep this a secret. Let's go do another Holy Spirit empowered small group!

Appendix C
A Word for Pastors and Small Group Leaders

DO WE AS leaders perceive *ourselves* as good gifts to others?

Many times people who visit our home group are too unhealthy to give much to those in attendance. As they experience love, acceptance, and forgiveness, however, one of the first signs of healing is a growing desire to reach out with an encouraging or uplifting word to someone else who is hurting.

This is the mutual edification of the body of Christ that Paul describes in 1 Corinthians 14:26: "How is it then, brethren? Whenever you come together, each of you has a psalm, has a teaching, has a tongue, has a revelation, has an interpretation. Let all things be done for edification."

LEADERSHIP EXPERIENCE

A small group will experience the presence of the Holy Spirit only to the depth to which the leader is comfortable with the process. Obviously, the leader must have experience in listening to and obeying the voice of the Spirit. The qualification necessary to lead a Holy Spirit empowered small group is being Holy Spirit empowered!

An empowered leader will exhibit a confidence for cooperating with the Holy Spirit, encouraging the group to join with what the Lord desires to do. He or she is able to listen for the cues and subtle leading as to what the Lord wants to do next. This requires experience.

How, then, do prospective leaders gain this valuable experience? It will depend on each leader's willingness to constantly pursue God until they are able to lead others into the viable presence of God. It will involve associating with Christians who are moving in the authentic anointing of God, as well as attending meetings where the Holy Spirit is allowed to minister. It will also involve ministry training that will result in a visible confidence and expectation that God will move in a group situation by healing and setting people free.

Ministry Training

Ministry Training Centers provide the kind of training in the local church institute that produces small group leaders who know what to do. They know how to create an environment where the Holy Spirit will most move in their midst. They know how to wait on God for instructions, and how to distinguish a work of the flesh from an authentic work of the Holy Spirit. They also know how to encourage those less acquainted with the moving of the Holy Spirit to simply enjoy what is going on. In addition, they know how to bring loving correction if it is needed.

Ministry Training Centers are centered in the dynamics of small group interaction. All of the practicum sessions are small group based. Twelve or fewer believers gather weekly to practice ministry skills and wait on God for prophetic words of encouragement and edification for each other. The more experienced leaders, who are graduates of MTC, direct and facilitate new practicum groups. By the end of the training, those so inclined are encouraged to begin leading a Holy Spirit empowered small group of their own. In this way, the small group network is continually expanding and being built up.

COOPERATING WITH THE HOLY SPIRIT

The benefits, release, and joy that flow from dynamic encounters with the Holy Spirit depend on the spiritual sensitivity of the leader, and his or her ability to sort out the weird from the authentic. Nothing spoils a meeting more than an over-zealous participant seizing a precious moment from the Holy Spirit and moving into the flesh. This is especially true when newcomers from other church backgrounds join a group. They may bring an unrestrained "everything goes" ministry protocol, assuming this is the way it is always done.

This is when firm and decisive leadership comes into play. Their actions may have been totally acceptable in their previously "free for all" environment. In these cases, we advise small group leaders to firmly step into the situation, touch the pause button, and use it as a teaching opportunity. When done in love, the group is relieved and can move back into the Spirit.

There is a false assumption pervading the body of Christ that whenever the Holy Spirit begins to do things in a group context, we must assume that whatever follows is also of the Holy Spirit. Paul warns us in 1 Corinthians to be discerning, and to insure that what transpires brings edification and not confusion to those gathered.

> God is not the author of confusion but of peace, as in all the churches of the saints.
> —1 CORINTHIANS 14:33

Some of the antics attributed to the Holy Spirit produce confusion. When confusion is allowed into a small group, everyone senses it (except, perhaps, the ones causing it). In such cases, the Holy Spirit lifts His presence as the people look around and wait for the leader to intervene. The tragedy comes when the leader just smiles and ascribes a work of the flesh to the Holy Spirit. They may say, "It's okay, we don't want to quench the Spirit. Let's move on."

What may have been considered authentic in one gathering may be totally out of order in another. An experienced small group leader will immediately discern an appropriate response within the group, and encourage the participants to flow with what is happening.

The maturity level of the majority of members should be kept in mind. If the group has not experienced the peculiar manifestations that are unique to other charismatic groups, e.g., falling under the power, holy laughter, and/or dancing in the Spirit, it would be totally inappropriate to encourage these to take place if that is not consistent with your group's vision.

RELEASING SUPERNATURAL GIFTS

Leaders set the pace in any meeting. Whatever they allow (or disallow) in the gathering is often viewed as "the" way you do it. It is critical that leaders make sure the supernatural gifts of the Holy Spirit are released in a *biblical* way.

Let's review a biblical approach to releasing the gifts in a group setting. First and foremost, the Lord Jesus Christ should be exalted in whatever transpires. The Holy Spirit always lifts up and honors the Lord Jesus. Anything that draws attention to an individual rather than the Lord is always suspect.

The following supernatural gifts listed in 1 Corinthians 12:4–11 should be regularly released in Holy Spirit empowered small groups:

The word of knowledge

This gift allows a believer to know something from God's perspective that has happened or is happening relating to a person or group of people. When allowed within the meeting, it will clarify what the Lord wants to do within the group. It will point out people needing divine direction, prayer, healing, or release. When the one receiving it speaks the word to the one for whom it is intended, the meeting has just been relinquished to the Holy Spirit. There will be a corporate witness and excitement for what will happen next.

The word of wisdom

This gift allows a believer to know God's plan and purpose for the lives of individuals within the group, or perhaps where God wants to take a meeting on a given evening. In such instances, God is revealing ahead of time what He wants to do. The wise group leader will immediately obey by speaking what he or she is hearing and do what God is revealing. The word of knowledge may reveal a particular person's need of healing. The word of wisdom will reveal exactly when and how to pray for the person. These two gifts will most often take place at the same time.

The discerning of spirits

This gift allows a believer to be aware of spirits, either good or bad, that may be around or on people. God may also use this gift to reveal His presence in such a way that everyone is struck with the fear of the Lord. This gift is very helpful to a leader when new people show up for the group meeting. By praying in the Spirit and asking the Lord for His insight, He may reveal a spirit that is behind certain individuals and the way they are attempting to pray for people. Small group leaders need to acquire experience in this gift for the protection of the group from wolves in sheep's clothing.

This gift is required to proceed in prayer for deliverance issues.

Healing

Always welcomed in a small group, this gift is the supernatural release of God's power and presence to heal the sick. It can happen through any believer who is expectant and desirous to pray for the healing of others. The Word of God has already authorized and empowered every believer to administer healing to those coming to God for healing.

Whenever the Lord gives a word of knowledge or wisdom regarding healing, quickly pray for the person and watch what God does. We have discovered that when God's revelation is involved, that means He wants to heal the person at that moment.

Faith

The supernatural gift of faith follows the revelation gifts of words of knowledge, wisdom, and discerning of spirits. Whenever a believer knows by revelation what God is about to do, there is supernatural faith that comes upon the believer to accomplish the miracle. In other words, he or she has complete trust in God that He will definitely accomplish what He just revealed.

The prudent leader will use the occasion to do a brief teaching on the gift of faith, and how it was sparked into operation by a word of knowledge or wisdom. The best classroom for learning about the gifts of the Spirit is right where they take place in a Holy Spirit empowered small group.

Prophecy

This gift encourages a believer to speak Holy Spirit-inspired words that will edify, exhort, or comfort those gathered. It can be a short phrase or an extended message. A word of prophecy will sometimes shift the agenda of the small group to a different focus such as healing, praying in the Spirit, worshiping, or referring to specific Scriptures that confirm the direction people are sensing. The gift of prophecy is always welcomed as an added dimension of the spontaneity of the Holy Spirit. Group leaders should always be ready to critique the words spoken by asking those for whom the word was intended if the word fit their situation. By so doing, it allows the words to be confirmed as either being from God or not. This can be a great learning situation for everyone attending the small group. When done properly, prophecy adds excitement and expectation for whatever God is attempting to communicate to the group.

All of this will be good material for you to go over with the apprentice home group leaders that you are raising up. Believe us when we say this is an exciting adventure upon which you are embarking!

Appendix D
Establishing a Ministry Training Center

W HEN A CHURCH decides to develop a network of Holy Spirit empowered small groups, it will, by necessity, require the group leaders to function confidently in the power of the Holy Spirit. To be successful, these leaders need to be trained to move with the Holy Spirit's leading. The best way to train small group leaders is to have them experience this in a small group atmosphere over many months. We recommend doing this kind of training in a mentoring-type environment where experienced trainers show potential small group leaders how to cooperate with the spontaneous agenda of the Holy Spirit.

We have developed the Ministry Training Centers to do this.

EVERY CHURCH IS A TRAINING CENTER

The local church is the logical place to begin training Christians to become effective small group leaders. Starting with the ministry basics of learning how to share Christ and praying for believers to be baptized in the Holy Spirit, the training also includes knowing how to pray for the sick. Advanced training would include how to hear from God, flow with the leading of the Holy Spirit, and set people free from spiritual bondages.

Over the last twenty years, we have proven this can be done without disciples becoming weird or "over the top." Ministry Training Centers (MTC) produce biblically-instructed lay ministers who can relieve the salaried staff by assuming most of the discipleship training functions. They do this as they step into leadership roles in a network of small groups.

It is a major decision for pastors to begin training members to operate in the supernatural. Many pastors want to avoid the excesses of out-of-control meetings, and activities that have no basis in Scripture. Such excesses can be avoided when the training is biblical, well thought out, high quality, practical, and totally reproducible.

To be effective, the training must include a balance of sound theology, while giving multiple opportunities for every student to experience hands-on ministry in a small group setting. Everything should be done under the watchful eyes of mature trainers, who can discern the difference between authentic manifestations of the Holy Spirit and off-the-chart weirdness.

Using the authors' three-volume Ambassador Series and their book, *Doing What Jesus Did*, local churches can establish a Ministry Training Center (MTC). It is remarkable that the curriculum works for a meeting place in third world countries, as well as mega-churches in America, and everything in between. We attribute this to the Holy Spirit's influence and anointing that accompany the teaching and hands-on practicum training sessions.

GATHER AN EQUIPPING TEAM

We recommend that the senior pastor *not* be the one who runs the MTC, especially in larger churches. He or she is already too busy. We do recommend that the senior pastor be a part of the MTC equipping team. The team must agree on a vision for training people to do what Jesus did.

Teachers with experience and a hunger for operating in supernatural ministry obviously make the best trainers. Though hard to find, they exist throughout the body of Christ. Retired or returning missionaries can be a terrific resource. Being trained by leaders in the local church who already operate in the supernatural of God is the quickest and best way to transfer the same anointing to those being trained.

This is how we train MTC small group leaders. The students start doing what their trainers have been doing in the safety of a small group environment. This, we believe, is how Jesus trained the first small group of disciples. And the same technique works in the twenty-first century.

First, the twelve watched Jesus do it. Then, they helped Jesus do it. Next, Jesus watched as they did it. Finally, they did it when Jesus was no longer with them. Today, we call this mentoring.

Train the Trainers

MTC offers a quick-start procedure for training small group leaders who have a desire to be part of the churches' discipleship process. Leaders and potential leaders are encouraged to attend a two-day, "Teacher Intensive." The "train-the-trainer" Teacher Intensive is designed for pastors, teachers, and leaders who have a heart for effective discipleship.

On a Friday night and Saturday, leaders are shown how to teach the Ambassador Series and conduct the six ministry skills from *Doing What Jesus Did*. The leaders are then authorized to order and teach the curriculum. Audiotapes and/or CDs of the three-volume Ambassador Series are available as teaching aids for the equipping team. The recordings are reviewed prior to teaching the lessons and are full of teaching tips and ideas to make the curriculum come alive.

Administrative and practicum guides are made available to the equipping team so they can put together a successful MTC. Any leader, pastor, or teacher who has attended a Teacher Intensive will be equipped to oversee or conduct an enduring MTC.

A Nine Month MTC

We recommend a nine-month schedule for an MTC. In the USA, it should be offered concurrent with the school year (September-May) with a graduation immediately following. The three-hour, once-a-week class is offered in an evening format.

Pastors often wonder if people are willing to make such a long commitment. We have addressed this issue by having students commit to twelve weeks (one quarter) at a time. By the time they have finished the first twelve weeks, you can't keep them away! Because of the exciting hands-on ministry skill sessions at MTC, we experience very little attrition through the year. Graduation is a special time where students receive a formal diploma in Practical Ministry, along with the laying on of hands and being commissioned as ambassadors for Christ.

The MTCs worldwide are doing what Jesus did. The classes are structured for maximum effectiveness. MTC trains the trainers how to train others within a small group environment.

Effective discipleship must be more than a teacher conducting classes where students take notes. True discipleship is an experienced mentor personally working side-by-side with a small group of disciples. They are ready when they know what the mentor knows and can do what the mentor can do. That is how Jesus did it. MTC functions the same way.

A Typical Class Session

Worship and teaching

First, fifteen minutes of strong worship to the Lord helps put everyone into the right frame of mind. Second, the trainers teach two forty-five minute lessons on the many facets of living the abundant life in Christ, obeying God's Word, and doing marketplace ministry. Every student receives a comprehensive training manual where he or she records personal illustrations so they can re-teach the lesson in the future.

Divide into small practicum groups

Between lessons, the entire class divides into small groups of ten or less, where every student practices the assigned ministry skill. Two students each week are scheduled to demonstrate the particular ministry skill. At the end of six weeks, the students are scheduled to demonstrate the next ministry skill. This is done until every disciple feels confident to attempt the skills in the marketplace.

Over thirty-six weeks, all six ministry skills are practiced and mastered: leading people to Christ, leading Christians into the Holy Spirit baptism, healing the sick, hearing from God, healing the sick by revelation, and dealing with demons.

An optional preaching practicum is offered for those preparing for public ministry.

Everyone receives ministry

The highlight of the weekly gathering is each student knowing he or she will both give and receive one-on-one prayer ministry within a small group of fellow students.

When it is time for a student to demonstrate the assigned ministry skill, it is done within the group, with a trained leader present. Afterward, they can request personal ministry for current needs. The others are encouraged to respond and pray over the person attempting to follow the Holy Spirit's leading. The Holy Spirit will often reveal Himself in profound ways, using another student through whom revelation or healing will take place.

Everyone gets to minister and receive ministry. Everyone goes home praising God for what they have personally experienced each week. The love quotient and bonding produced in these training sessions are amazing. It produces true, biblical koinonia.

Go do it for real

In order to graduate and receive a diploma in Practical Ministry, every student minister must demonstrate that they can do all six ministry skills. The final "exam" requires each student minister to take what he or she has learned and "do it for real" in the marketplace. They must make two attempts to lead someone to Christ, two attempts to lead believers into the Holy Spirit baptism, and two attempts to heal the sick. All of the attempts must be done outside of the classroom in a small group gathering or in the marketplace.

Confidence is catching

During the last month of training, the testimonies of doing what Jesus did "for real" start coming in. Student after student gives spontaneous reports of healings, deliverances, and various miracles as they "attempted" to fulfill the outside-of-class assignments. It always brings a smile to the instructors when they hear exciting testimonies of how the Holy Spirit "took over" the attempt and turned it into a genuine "doing what Jesus did" success story.

The final step

Months before, these Christian "laymen" were ineffective and even fearful of reaching out in the name of Christ. By this time, they are going into their part of the world and doing greater things for God than they ever dreamed possible. The graduates of MTC are prepared to take the final step. They are strongly encouraged to start or join a Holy Spirit empowered small group. This is where they can "do it for real" everything they learned in the MTC.

When a small group has six of these kinds of fully devoted and trained disciples, the excitement and enthusiasm are catching. Guests sense the presence of God and during the ministry time exciting things start happening.

How to Get Started

Trainers must experience the MTC mentoring dynamic. The hands-on practicum is the heart of the training and cannot be learned by reading a book. We have developed the fast-paced MTC Teacher Intensive so pastors and leaders can experience how to conduct the ministry skill sessions. Teacher aids and suggestions are available for teachers to start an exciting MTC in their church.

The MTC Teacher Intensive

We cannot improve on Jesus' strategy for training believers. He put His life into a small group of "trainers" who turned the world upside down. Here is how it is done:

- MTC will "train the trainers" in regional Teacher Intensives. These are open to any active leader involved in pastoring, teaching, evangelizing, or missionary work.

- The pastor of an established church must initiate the inquiry for hosting the Teacher Intensive.

- Tentative dates, seminar location, and costs for hosting a regional Teacher Intensive are negotiated and agreed upon with the host church.

- Other pastors in the region with a vision for this kind of ministry training are contacted and invited to participate.

- Once a final estimate of participating churches and attendees is confirmed, a firm date and training location are established.

- Updates, costs, and other details are available through the website: www.ministrytraining.org.

A Personal Invitation

If you have read this far, you undoubtedly know that our (John and Sonja's) passion is to see the body of Christ equipped to do what Jesus did. We are assisting pastors in establishing MTCs in local churches around the globe. Please contact the MTC offices if you are interested in learning how to start an MTC by attending an MTC Teacher Intensive. We hold Teacher Intensives here in Bend, Oregon at our local church and also schedule the training by direct invitation from senior pastors. If you are a pastor that has read this book and are interested in pursuing ministry training, you are invited to contact the MTC offices.

Planning will then begin for a weekend training session in your region. We would consider it a privilege and an honor to serve pastors of local churches anywhere in the world! For more information, contact us at mtc@ministrytraining.org.

Appendix E
Mobilizing Untapped Resources

As we mentioned earlier in the book, there are vast untapped people-resources sitting in the pews of churches across the Christian world. These are people who need to be awakened, engaged, instructed, and mobilized. Pastors, here is a simple plan for doing this:

- Pray and ask the Holy Spirit for His involvement from the outset. How would He like to be presented in your church?

- After getting a go-ahead from the Lord, solicit enthusiastic support from your staff, church council, and non-salaried leadership.

- Insert a flyer in your weekly bulletin that announces a one-hour meeting to explain about a plan to introduce more of the Holy Spirit into the life of the congregation through home groups. Use verbiage like: "If you are interested in learning about the Holy Spirit, His gifts, fruit, etc., this will be of interest to you."

If your church is a candidate for launching a Ministry Training Center, this would be a great way to train inexperienced Christians in the things of the Spirit and to retool the experienced folks by making sure their theology is sound. The MTCs are small-group based for the practicum sessions, so they can be observed in ministry situations while they practice the six ministry skills:

1. Leading people to Christ

2. Leading Christians into the Holy Spirit baptism

3. Learning how to heal the sick

4. Hearing from God

5. Healing the sick by revelation

6. Dealing with demons.

We find that many Christians have large gaps in their theology, and the MTC lays a solid foundation in their lives. It also allows any old-fashioned ways of prophesying in King James English to be updated to a more relevant presentation. (Appendix D tells how to establish a Ministry Training Center.)

Let us know if we can assist you.

To order additional copies online: www.ministrytraining.org. Or call toll free: 1-877-866-9406.

1 407 394 9169

Notes

INTRODUCTION

1. For a teaching on this biblical experience, please refer to Appendix A.

Chapter 2

LET'S DO IT JESUS' WAY

1. Judy's remarkable story is recounted in chapter six.

Chapter 3

SMALL GROUP ANATOMY

1. Appendix C, "A Word for Pastors and Small Group Leaders," defines these gifts and how they should be released in the small group dynamic.
2. See Appendix D, "How to Establish a Ministry Training Center."

Appendix B

THIRTEEN-WEEK SMALL GROUP STUDY

1. Our Ministry Training Centers (MTCs) produce these kinds of group leaders who can lead these dynamic, Holy Spirit empowered small groups. (See Appendix D for a step-by-step way to do this.)

407 - 271 - 1373